W9-AFE-766

Under New Management

Also by Sam Shoemaker

EXTRAORDINARY LIVING FOR ORDINARY MEN

Under New Management

by Sam Shoemaker

ZONDERVAN PUBLISHING HOUSE
GRAND RAPIDS, MICHIGAN

UNDER NEW MANAGEMENT

Library of Congress Catalog Card Number 66-28236

First printing 1966
Second printing 1967
Third printing 1968
Fourth printing 1969
Fifth printing January 1970
Sixth printing June 1970

Printed in the United States of America

ABOUT THE BOOK

Sam Shoemaker left a rich spiritual and literary legacy. He wrote more than two dozen books and countless articles, and at the time of his death in 1963 there were in the files of *Faith at Work* magazine literally hundreds of sermons, radio scripts and articles, many of which had never appeared in print. It is from these sources that *Under New Management* has come. In some cases, transitional sentences have been added at the ends of chapters, but otherwise the words are all Sam's. The manuscript has been prepared and edited by Richard Engquist and the staff of *Faith at Work.*

Contents

I. Living is EXPERIMENT

1.

ARE WE SPECTATORS OR PARTICIPANTS?

THERE ARE VARIOUS WAYS in which you can think of the Christian religion. You can view it as a complex system of theological beliefs. You can see it as a system of ethics—a profound simplification of the moral experience of mankind. You can think of it as a way of life, concerned with the spirit in which one lives day by day.

All of these are true, but none of them gives any idea of what a Christian life is really like. In the same way you might say of a man that he is six feet tall, has four children, likes to play tennis, works in a hardware store—all these things may be true and important, but they give you only the least inkling of what the man is really like.

The Christian religion is only to be defined in terms of *life*, not in terms of words or concepts. Words seem to invite dispute; they may confuse us or leave us cold. But life—well, there it is. Be with it, watch it—and you will soon learn what it is.

Christianity is such a fascinating thing. We all know that, if it is true, it is really the one thing that unlocks the mystery of life. For it comes from the "other side," and is revelation. Hence we find ourselves almost unable to stay away from it.

Many of those who wouldn't think of calling themselves Christians nevertheless wonder what Christianity is all about;

whether it might have meaning for them, provide answers to their questions and a more satisfying style of life. More and more people today are reading and seeking and experimenting. But if they should come to church to seek, will they find us pursuing something that seems complicated, dull, or meaningless? Will they hear words that have no root in their experience?

On the other hand they may come to love and enjoy the words of the service, the familiar words of Scripture, the old hymn-tunes, the beauty of the church building, and the stained glass windows. These things may help to enrich a real and living faith, but they may also provide a false substitute for it. The formal pursuit of religion may positively deaden spiritual sensibilities. Worship has no meaning coming from a heart withheld from God.

The result is that some of us are like people watching others play a game. We are not down on the field, running and sweating and trying to make a point—we are comfortably watching a kind of religious TV show where others are the participants. If this is true, perhaps it is because we have genuinely misunderstood what Christianity is about and how it means to deal with human nature. Or, perhaps, we are just plain lazy and do not want religion to disturb the comfort of our routine respectability.

For myself, I visualize Christianity as a stream of power coming from God, through Christ, through the Church, to people. This power is called *grace.*

Grace means the favor and goodness of God, especially as this is extended to people who do not deserve it. Much grace comes directly to open hearts that seek God. We cannot see it, except in its effects. We cannot take it in our hands, though we can willfully turn off its power. It is like the air we breathe—but the soul must be open to it as the lungs are open to air.

You have perhaps come under the sway of a personality

who had something you needed and wanted—a teacher who fed your mind, a friend who gave you the companionship you needed, a person of faith and wide experience who helped you deal with pressing problems. You felt the impact of a whole personality. You felt the human counterpart to "grace" in men.

Grace is God's influence and impact on us, His power sent out to us. When we pray and are still long enough, when we seek God, not for anything He can do for us, but just for Himself, we are aware that we are in an outgoing stream of influence, power, love. The whole purpose of faith is to get us into that stream and keep us there! It is not only to make us believe certain doctrines, though they are true; nor to stand by certain principles, though they are right. It is to get us into the stream of God's love and power and grace. For we can never do for ourselves what needs to be done; only God can do it for us.

Let me give you what I believe are some of the steps by which people come into that stream of God's power.

(1) Usually we see it in others. They may stand deep in a profound stream of it, or they may just wade in a shallow one—but there is water there and we know it. They may be fairly ordinary church-goers without much pretense to great holiness; but they go regularly, and it gives them a stability and a little more peace than most people have access to.

Some of them are remarkable people. Not one of us but has seen a few real Christian saints in whose lives is a radiant and radiating power. They meet trouble and pain with God-given victory. They are patient with the sins of others. They will take real trouble for people. They know very well that any power in them comes *to* them, not *from* them.

The outstanding ones are not too many, but we never know where we're going to run across one of them. Whether they have a lot of grace or only a little of it, we recognize it. And that makes us envy it. And that may start the process of our own search for it.

(2) We must be open to the stream of God's power. Some people come where it is, but do not open themselves to it. As if a man should go into a shower bath with rubber boots, a raincoat and a sou'wester' hat on—he will come out as dry as he went in. The world is full of buttoned-up people. They do not smile, they do not speak, they take no part in singing the hymns nor making the responses during the service. They imprison themselves in a dungeon of self-consciousness.

We shall often need to get into the stream of some human fellowship before we find the stream of God's power. You may need to try to make friends with others in God's family before you will be open to coming into it yourself. God wants you in it, and His people do. But you must make some effort yourself to open yourself to Him and the stream of His power.

(3) You need an increasing belief that this *can happen to you.* As we see others to whom God means something we are likely to say, "She was always like that," or "I could never have what he has." Such a reaction turns off the stream of power as definitely as you turn off the water in a spigot with your hand. Remember, God wants you in the stream of His love and power. He made you for this purpose, and your life has no meaning so great as this.

You may need to break old molds of thought about yourself. You may need to scrap the false pictures of yourself you've been showing to the world. Start relaxing the muscles of your face! Drop the tension that puts you on good behavior. Send out some wavelengths of friendliness and human warmth. Seek out someone who feels more strange and self-conscious than you. Let God get your heart open to receiving from Him what He wants you to have—not a stiff belief, not a code of ethics only, not some kind of piety you put on when you come to church, but His surrounding love and grace. God wants us, I am sure, to meet Him in His church. But churchgoing needs to affect our bodies, our feelings, our minds, our human relations—everything.

(4) Step into the stream! God is wanting you and drawing you, exactly as you want your little son to get up and take his first steps, and you give him your hand.

Two things may make you hesitate: the fear that you will not "stick with it," or something you don't want to give up. You know you can't be fully in the stream of this world, with its many false values, and also in the stream of God's grace, even though you'd like to be in both. But how little do the things we give up appear, after the great experience has happened!

You may feel a bit awkward slithering down the bank where you have been sitting for so long, first getting your toes wet, and then slowly getting wet all over. There is no swimming for people who only wade, and there is no enjoying the full stream of the grace of God for those who hang onto the roots and bushes on the bank and never let themselves go.

Let yourself go entirely. Let the water in the stream hold you up, instead of relying on your will power. Reservations and delays and sins have held you back long enough. Get in, and let the stream of the grace of God wash and buoy and carry you along. Let self-effort drown beneath those waters!

(5) Keep in the stream. All of us step out of the stream at times, when we go back to our own way, when we hurt someone by selfishness, or hurt God by disobedience. But living in that stream can become as much our natural habitat as water is for a fish. Once we have "tasted and seen how good the Lord is," we feel miserable when we are not close to Him. The reason why many are content to be spectators

and not participants is that they have never known how wonderful life could be, living in that stream.

Prayer is the main thing that keeps us in the stream. Prayer ought to fill every chink of time we have. There is immense help also in gathering in God's house, especially for Holy Communion. But prayer can go with us wherever we go. When we step out of the stream by a hasty word, or a wrong decision, or a selfish reaction, and realize it promptly, we can as quickly ask God for forgiveness and step back again into the stream.

Let me go on to say three more things.

The stream is, I believe, the steady work of the Holy Spirit of God. There are people who like to say that they "tap" sources of power in a metaphysical way, as if all this were an impersonal force, like gas or electricity. God is very good, and rewards all honest search for Him, often in very wonderful ways. The question is, however, where does the power come from? If it comes from my right attitudes it is really self-generated, even though I may have called on those metaphysical forces. But if it comes from without, as I believe it does when it is genuine, then there must be an outside source. That source is the Holy Spirit. This is not a theological fine point. The deepest question is whether we use God, or whether we ask God to use us. There is a time of immaturity when we do use God, just as little children use us; but maturity means cooperation between children and parents, and spiritual maturity means that we seek God's will, not our own.

We are held up by the buoyancy of the stream itself. We commit ourselves to God as a ship commits itself to the ocean. This is the basic leap of faith. So much steel as is in the liner, rolled up together and thrown into the water, would sink. Some people feel that when they throw themselves into the stream of God's grace, there will be nothing there, and they will sink. Nothing can disprove this except the experiment of faith itself. When we leap clear, we find we are buoyed. This is the experience of grace, and no one who has had it, doubts it. We exert only the effort of opening our hearts and our hands to grace, that we may receive it. The rest is God's work.

The mark of grace is found in certain things that happen to those who are in the stream of it. Let me caution against seeking to get what you want by coming into the stream of grace. That is always a dangerous thing to do. But if there are no events in our lives which we incline to call "coincidences," and maybe later "miracles," there is a question whether we are in the life or out of it. At the end of St. Mark's gospel are these words, "And they went forth and preached everywhere, while the Lord worked with them and confirmed the message by the signs that attended it." Those "signs" are very real. We cannot produce them, but God lets them happen. Life is freer, happier, more coordinated, more in relation to other lives than it ever was. And we are not to be surprised if that stream leads one day to a place called Calvary, where we shall undergo some crucifixion as our Lord did. Being in grace is no guarantee against trouble and difficulty, though it is a guarantee against defeat and rebellion. The people in grace that I know have things "happen" to them that they consider extraordinary and even miraculous, as if the other world impinged on this one, as if the heavenly forces were at work in the earth.

This is part of the Christian experience, and part of our birthright. Do these things happen to you? Are they happening without your seeing and recognizing them? Do you need to come right down into the stream, so that God can give you all He wants you to have? Let us see how this can happen.

2.

A KNOTTY BUSINESS AND A "NAUGHTY" WORD

NOWADAYS THE WORD CONVERSION scares the wits out of most people. To the modern sophisticate, it brings to mind a weird and vaguely unhealthy flight from reality. To many churchgoers, it smacks of tent meetings, ignorance, and emotionalism. But no one can look into the question of religion without knowing that conversion is a very great reality and a very great necessity. When Jesus says, "You must be born again," we are hearing from Him an inescapable imperative.

Many of us in churches try to push this imperative from us. We think that if we were born of decent people and have grown up in the Church, we do not need to hear about conversion. Yet Jesus had His worst trouble not with those on the "outside," who were far from God and knew it, but with those "inside," who were far from God and did *not* know it.

Pharisees occur in every religion in every age. They are the self-satisfied who do not wish to face themselves as they really are in the sight of God, and who resist whatever reminds them of their failures and sins. So, whether we are in the Church or out of it, conversion ought to be a live and burning issue for us.

Conversion is the first step into the stream of God's grace —the stream of life as it is meant to be lived. But what is it?

The really converted person has at some time faced the great need of his life and realized that he was powerless to help himself. He then turned to God, "not as a gentleman in search of religion, but as a sinner in search of salvation."

This tremendous event, then, begins with a sense of *need.* The Pharisee can never think of anything so heinous in his life that he needs redemption in this desperate way. All he looks for is fortification to keep on being as good as he is. For him, such a thing as conversion is nonsense. But for those of us who are dissatisfied, fed up with ourselves, "lost," it provides an option of cataclysmic power.

I believe there are two needs in every life. There is the sin that gets us into trouble—the willfulness, the immorality, the lawlessness. There is also the pride that makes one determined to work things out by himself, without any breaking-down, without any appeal to other human beings for help, and without any turning to God other than repeating prayers and going to church in the usual way.

Pride is every man's "other sin." We each have our characteristic failures—impatience, irritability, self-indulgence; but behind them is the ever-present spectre of pride, deeper, more subtle, infinitely more sinful than any other. Our grossest, most obvious weaknesses are really just a front for pride. Pride is what is the matter with all of us.

The thing that Alcoholics Anonymous does for people is to reach and begin to cure their pride. Alcoholism is not the chief problem, big as it is. In AA, a man admits he is an alcoholic and needs help from God and from other people. If he is not willing to make such an admission, he is "too good" to join up with AA.

Most of us, while we have plenty of our own kinds of sins, feel a bit superior to such people as alcoholics, or anyone else who gets into outward difficulty. That is why we "Pharisees" never feel any affinity with the "prodigals," and why we can't be of much use to them. We do not really *feel* like sinners at all. But, in heaven's name, who are we to feel superior to someone whose sins are merely disreputable, when our own may be absolutely disastrous?

Therefore the thing from which we must be converted is not alone, and not so much, the bad temper or lust or drunkenness or cruelty or laziness which may be our *obvious* sin, but the pride which is our *hidden* sin—hidden to ourselves, but plain as a signboard to the rest of the world!

The good family man, the noble citizen, the generous philanthropist, the benevolent dictator in the home (and his inevitable counterpart, the doormat), can be positively eaten up with pride. They usually are. People tell them how wonderful they are, and they tell themselves the same thing. Therefore they never get wise to themselves, and never put themselves within range of getting converted.

Pride tells us to do everything ourselves—including getting rid of our sins. But the cross of Christ tells us that we simply cannot do anything of the kind. God's way is to be broken Himself, in order that we may see that something needs to be broken in us.

What gets broken is our pride. For this greatly needed redemption—of which respectable people need to be made aware far more than disreputable people, who already know they can't "go it alone"—can only be accomplished by One greater than we. This is what gets at our pride, and begins to kill it. We must come to God simply and humbly in our need.

When we do this, we begin to be converted. For somehow, when you stand before Christ on His cross, it is pretty hard to tell Him how good you are, and how little you need, and how unnecessary in your case it was for Him to go through that agony and shame. All you can do is to bow your head, and accept.

As we come to see what God did for us in Christ, we begin to see our own righteousness as "filthy rags," and God's redemption as our one last hope. Something melts down within us. We begin to thank Him for every event and for every person who has helped us to this desperation. Something dies in us, and the new life in Christ begins to take its place.

We cannot ooze into such a great relationship; we must make ourselves a party to it. Jesus Christ offers it to us. We must accept—or reject.

The human situation is that conversion, which begins in an *act*, is also a *process*; and because we are human, it is a zigzag and sometimes intermittent one. Being converted is something like being married—we are committed for life to one person. But this does not mean we become at our marriage a perfect husband or wife. We spend the rest of our lives working out that commitment, sometimes with success, sometimes with failure.

In marriage, two fallible human beings are involved. In conversion, one fallible human being and one infallible and divine Being are involved. He never fails us, but we fail Him very often. We are beginning to be converted when we stop excusing and justifying our repeated failures, and admit that they are the outcropping of sides of our nature that still need to be redeemed.

Conversion thus has two meanings. It means a continuous effort to live in Christ and for Him and by His help, seeking to strengthen and deepen our original decision. It also means the honest awareness that our lives repeatedly fall far below that original commitment and decision, and have to be brought back to God for forgiveness and renewal.

This implies a delicate balance. Some of us are far too patient with ourselves, in that we do not work strenuously at our continued conversion. Others demand of themselves, and then of others, a perfectionism that may be very full of pride, as if to say, "Maybe others will fail Christ, but I will not." Peter said something like that just before his great denial.

I believe profoundly in the reality of the original decision and self-surrender. It is as final, but also as incomplete, as the promises one makes to his beloved in the wedding ceremony. It has to be done, and many of us in the Church have never really done it.

But I grow increasingly leery of people who have no hesitation in calling themselves "surrendered, born-again Christians." I can say that of a good many people I know, but I cannot say it of myself except with the reservations I have mentioned. I hope and believe I am in a kind of crucible of redemption, in which the slag is getting burned out that the metal may survive.

"But wait," you say, "you were going to tell how to get into the stream of life, and now you're all hung up on 'conversion to Christ!' Back up a minute, and stop tossing about those theological phrases."

Fair enough. Let us look at one example of conversion and see what its elements may be.

And, to be as fair as possible, let me tell you what happened in my own life.

3.

TURNABOUT—A PERSONAL STORY

IN 1918 I WAS IN OLD PEKING, CHINA. It was wartime. I had agreed to go out on short term to teach in a school supported by Princeton University, where Chinese lads learned the rudiments of English and business methods.

Besides my teaching in the business school, I was given a class of young businessmen who were inquirers into the Christian faith. We gathered in my room around a stove on cold autumn evenings. The first time there were about twenty, the next about fourteen, and the third about seven. I was becoming aware that something was the matter with that inquirers' class! I suspected that it was not only my ignorance of how to teach.

I had been brought up in a responsible, conservative, churchgoing Episcopalian family. My early associations were happy and valuable, and enough to dispose me toward a great interest in religion and to a decision to enter the ministry. I began lay-reading at seventeen, conducting services for the men who worked on my father's place in Maryland. As a senior at Princeton, I was president of the Christian Association.

But it is one thing to be interested in religion, and even to conduct services or to feel called to the ministry; it is quite another thing to be able to communicate your faith to others. So a great sense of failure overtook me in Peking with that dwindling class of inquirers.

About that time, some people came to Peking who brought with them spiritual power. I was caught by their contagious joy and effectiveness.

Thinking of one very intelligent and promising young man in my inquirers' class who seemed more interested in Christianity than the others, I said to myself, "Here are the very people to get hold of him!" So I went round and asked the leader of this company if he would see this man and try to win him for Christ.

Without the least hesitation, he said, "Why don't you win him yourself?" I replied that I was an Episcopalian, and we did not go in much for this sort of thing. I should not like to jump in on such delicate work as this, any more than I should begin with a penknife to operate on a man for appendicitis.

He said to me, "Now what do you think is the *real* reason?"

I countered by asking him what he thought the real reason was. Quick as a flash he said, "Might be sin."

That Saturday I went home with what Studdert-Kennedy calls "a pain in the mind." As I knelt down to say my prayers, somehow everything "jammed." My words didn't seem to get as high as the ceiling, and I knew that I was up against my Waterloo. Either I would or would not "let go," so far as I understood God and His will.

For, while I was decided about the ministry, and was then a teacher in China on short term, I knew I had not faced the issue of the mission field for life. A couple of years was fascinating, but a lifetime out there? That was something else.

It seemed to me I heard Somebody saying, "You want to do my work in *your* way." There were some other things to be cleared up as well, such as one deep resentment. I knew that I could not even pray, let alone give God a chance to use me to win someone else, until I "let go."

I looked into the mirror, shook a finger at myself, and said,

"You've got to come across or you've got to go home. You are out here under false pretenses." Then, with much more will than emotion, I knelt down beside my desk, and one by one let go of the things I knew were standing between me and God, and between me and other people. The crux of it was my willingness to stay in China all my life if God should will it. As in the story of Abraham and Isaac, the willingness was the important thing.

I felt no great emotion. I think I did feel that my life had slipped into the place where it belonged.

The next morning I woke up with the uneasy feeling that somehow I must go and talk to my young Chinese businessman friend. That afternoon I got into a ricksha and drove the three miles to where he lived. Pacing up and down outside his door, I almost prayed he would not be at home, but when I finally rapped he called, "Come in."

My heart sank. As I crossed the threshold, I asked God what on earth I was to say, and it came to me to tell what had happened to me the night before. When I did, he said, "I wish that could happen to me." I said, "It can. Just be honest with God about your needs and ask Him to come in and take over your life." We talked about our sins, and we talked about Jesus Christ and His love and power. That day the young man made his decision and found Christ.

That is perhaps not the kind of "conversion story" you expected to hear. It doesn't sound much like what happens at a Billy Graham crusade, or what is supposed to happen at confirmation. But it *is* a conversion story, and looking back I see that there were four elements that went into this initial spiritual decision.

(1) *The break with conscious wrong.* Someone has said that we "take hold of God by the handle of our sins." He comes to us, like a doctor, at the point of our need. If we have a bad temper, we must be willing to let it be controlled.

If we resent someone, we must be willing to replace the resentment with love.

To be sure, these surface sins will later uncover some that lie much deeper, but let us begin by trying to be honest with God about the things that are fouling up ourselves and our relationships—and let us be very specific.

(2) *The taking of time for personal devotions.* If the new life is to grow and continue, it must be fed. Set apart a regular time each day; pray for people, read the Bible. I'll never forget how much it helped me to look up every reference I could find to Peter, and discover in nearly every one of them weaknesses like my own; yet Christ called him a "rock" and greatly used him.

(3) *The necessity of putting life's major decisions in God's hands.* God wants to mold not only the spirit but also the locus of one's life. Marriage needs to be considered from the angle of God's will, not from human desire alone. Every young person needs to realize these things and act upon them. The will of God must become every man's North Star, to which he is continually adjusting the compass of his life.

(4) *The need to learn how to witness.* Most Christians are tongue-tied and unconvincing. Keep quiet about the trivia of your religion, and talk about its great elements—God, sin, conversion, grace, prayer. People will listen to you if you mix your experience with your convictions.

It is not shyness or humility that keeps us from expressing our faith, but cowardice and poverty of spiritual experience. From the first day until now, the great ongoing power of the Church has been its witness to its Lord.

I tell this story because I know how important it is *to begin.* Before a child can grow, he must be born. Before we can grow spiritually, we must be "born again." Growth is gradual; birth is sudden. It takes a long time for an oak tree to grow to maturity; it does not take long to put an acorn into the ground, knowing that the dampness and chemicals go to work at once to break the shell that the new life may begin.

Of course, everyone does not get started in the same way, but everyone needs to get started. When we feel and admit the need for some power outside ourselves; when we ask God (however we may understand Him) to take control of our lives; when we are willing to make the break with conscious wrong and to be open to a new understanding of God and other people—then we have taken that first leap into the stream of life.

Then the fun begins! The "fun" is the deep satisfaction of being truly alive, mixed with all the joy and pain of growth. It is the discovery of fantastic promises, and of principles that turn our old values upside-down.

Let us look at one such promise and one such principle.

4.

THE FACULTY OF FAITH

IN THE GOSPEL according to Matthew, chapter 7, verses 7 and 8, we find this amazing promise: "Ask, and it shall be given you; seek, and you will find; knock, and it will be opened to you. For every one who asks receives, and he who seeks finds, and to him who knocks it will be opened" (RSV).

Think about what kind of mentality, what kind of heart, what kind of life and personality stand behind these words of Jesus. He was fully human. What He said would not have been so close to life, so full of power to capture the imagination of people ever since, if it had not been wrought out of experience.

Jesus made this promise because it corresponded with the facts, and because it could be tested in experience. He said it because He knew people who worked on this principle and found it dependable. He worked on it Himself, and spoke out of His own experience.

Of course, He wrestled with evil, with unanswered prayer, with human disappointment, with the long waits life sometimes requires of us. But He began with faith as an axiom. And He gave us one of the richest possible interpretations of life.

At times He seems to have ignored the matter of theological or even ethical content, and just told people to throw themselves on the mercy of God, to go with the stream that flows through the universe, to trust utterly and absolutely, even to trust that their own desires would be close enough to the desires of God so that He could answer their prayers and bring about their fulfillment.

"Yes," you say, "but what about when Jesus prayed in Gethsemane, and asked God to spare Him the cross? That prayer wasn't answered."

I don't know what Jesus would say to that, but I have known some very profound believers in prayer in my lifetime, and I think I know how *they* would answer it. They would probably say two things: (1) You *receive* even when God's answer seems to be *No*—as Christ received, out there under the trees in the Garden of Gethsemane, the strength to meet the cross the next day. (2) For a person who flings himself on the mercy of God and trusts Him for everything, the overwhelming reality is the fulfillment of life. Life is enriched with the glory and wonder of finding that God works with us and uses us and guides us and gives us a part in His creation as it continues.

Yes, people who trust and obey in that fashion *do* receive, and find, and have doors opened to them. There are lapses, events hard to account for, times when prayer does not seem to work. But the great, overall quality of such a life is precisely the fulfillment He promises.

It is therefore immensely more important that we have *faith* than that we have *religion*. Many people have religion, but almost no faith at all. Others know very little about orthodox religion, but are full of faith.

Jesus certainly implied some gigantic theological claims concerning Himself, and I believe that Christian theology is an honest deduction from things He was and did and said and taught. We cannot, therefore, evade these intellectual realities. But neither can we forget that there were times when He seemed to put faith at the very top of the list, and to tell people that if they went for *that*, everything would work out for the best.

I am sure that the main job of the churches is to get dynamic faith across to people, so that they may live in the climate and power of these amazing words. The question is, how do we become people of faith?

First, I should say, let us not be too self-conscious about our search for faith. Let's not burrow too deeply into our motives in wanting it. They will almost certainly be mixed.

What mother or father expects a little child to be unselfish from the beginning? We grow toward unselfishness with our parents, and we grow toward it with God. Leave behind you, then, the self-consciousness which says, "Who am I to be looking for favors from God?" The answer is that you *are* His child, whether you act like it or not.

Don't say, "Oh, I could never be as faithful and loving as George or Mary!" Such an attitude undercuts faith from the very start, as if you put your heel on the green blade coming up from a planted seed, and squashed it down into nothingness.

You are a human being who needs God, as all of us do. Forget everything about yourself but your need.

Second, begin to steep yourself in the love and power of God. Go where people talk about Him. Read as much as you can that will dispose your mind toward faith.

God's love toward us is much more dependable than our love toward Him. He is with us, working in us, leading us into and through experiences we need, even when we are not at all conscious of it.

The world is full of those who believe, without reservation, that God is, and that He is love, and that He has power in Himself with which to help struggling, baffled people. They call on Him for help and He gives it. The more we associate with such people, the more of this faith rubs off on us. We "catch" it, like a contagion.

Third, do not circumscribe God's power by saying it must

come to you in a particular way. Many of us have envied the definiteness of another's religious experience. I believe God wants to come to you just as definitely, but He may want to do it in a different way.

A Lutheran minister I know traveled seventeen hundred miles to seek a conversion like his Methodist mother-in-law had. He admired her and her experience greatly. But he was reminded that God is not necessarily a Methodist! God gave him a rather quiet conversion, but a real one—I saw him twenty-five years later, still going strong.

Another man told me that at the time of his conversion from unbelief to faith in God, a blinding white light shone around him. But after that God seemed to lead him in quiet ways, sometimes not showing him until the last minute which way to go, and then with just the gentlest feeling to clarify the decision. The initiative lies with God all the time. All we have to do is to be open.

Fourth, we can do some things that may foster our own conversion, though we cannot finally cause it. The great verse is, "By grace you are saved, through faith."

Years ago, people often had a rain barrel at the corner of the house to catch the rain. Our "rain barrel" is openness, willingness. You get a clean, empty barrel—as clean and empty as you can make it—and you open it at the top so the rain can come in. It may stand there dry for days or weeks, but one day rain is going to come. If the top is off, and the barrel is open, some of the rain is surely going to pour in.

It is just so with the grace of God. In one sense, grace is around us all the time, just as there is always moisture in the air. But at times God gives us a "fall" of grace. We must not try to command such things, nor hurry them, nor fake them; but we must be open and ready for them.

Fifth, let faith be its own self-starter. Throw yourself on the mercy of God and of life. Try to realize that God is greater than you, and that He cares what happens to you.

Cry out your need to Him, and act as if He were caring for you.

Try to get yourself up off the ground, and above your doldrums and negatives and self-centeredness. Behave as if you believed, as if it were all true. Sometimes you have to shake a watch to get it to run. This is not spiritual self-deception, but spiritual experimentation.

Try the way of believing as against the way of not believing. More and more you will find yourself swept along in a current not of your own making. Life has purpose and meaning. The level of faith begins to rise. You wonder how you could ever have lived otherwise!

Now you are swimming strongly in the stream, at times resting and letting it carry you along with its own current. All goes well.

And then, one day, something happens. You seem to have hit a snag or a sandbar. You're not moving at all. What went wrong?

5.

FORM OR FORCE?

I SUPPOSE ALL OF US are more or less familiar with the process by which religion, begun as a force, turns into a form. A live message and movement burn in a man's soul. He draws other people about him who kindle to his vision. They band together and work as a group. They build up a body of experience and commonly accepted truth. They know its power, and want to transmit it to others.

When others join the group who have not known the days of its force, they give undue importance to this rescript of experience instead of maintaining the experience itself. And the first thing you know, you have on your hands a dead orthodoxy, a religion of remembrance, a tradition which has ceased to be an experience.

In Paul's final word to Timothy, his son in the faith, we find this contemporary-sounding prediction:

> There are hard times coming in the last days. For men will be selfish, fond of money, boastful, haughty, abusive, disobedient to their parents, ungrateful, irreverent, callous, relentless, scurrilous, dissolute, and savage; they will hate goodness, they will be treacherous, reckless and conceited, preferring pleasure to God—for though they keep up a form of religion they will have nothing to do with it as a force (II Timothy 3:1-5, Moffatt).

So if we get hung up on that snag, or marooned on that sandbar, and feel that the stream of life is passing us by, it may be that the force of our faith has degenerated into mere form. When this happens, there are two helpful things that we should keep in mind.

The first is that any movement which has God and truth in it, and which is loyal to what has been revealed, has in it also a strange power of self-renewal. Weak movements go to the wall and disappear. Strong ones die down, like perennials in winter, but come up again in another form at some later spring.

The vitality of movements must be tested, not by their power to ward off the experience of dying down—almost all of them go through this—but to survive. We do not get a dead-level of advance and progress, we get instead ups and downs. Something continues and keeps going that can be fanned by the Spirit into fresh life, if the original impulse came from God.

The second thing to remember is that form may be the channel of force. When you want to use electricity, you do not go out and try to catch lightning in a pail; you put wires in your house through which electricity runs. Wires are only forms. If the current is not on, they are as harmless and worthless as so many pieces of rope. But when the current is on, the form becomes the channel for the force.

The Church is meant to be a wire like that. But sometimes we cut the wire and the power is stopped. Or the Church becomes short-circuited by intolerance or hate, stopping the flow of God's sympathy toward all human beings by an unwillingness to extend its own sympathy so far.

Religion has its places of definite power. Prayer is one of them; when you plug in there, you get a result. Holy Communion is another. Fellowship is another; when you are in touch with other people possessing faith, it is like touching live wires.

We discover the reality of prayer only when we pray. Shakespeare's plays are nothing standing on a shelf; they come to life when we read them, and still more when we see great actors play them. Then the words which were only words become the channel of great understanding.

All this means that the important thing, even more important than the form, is the force. If people have been exposed only to the form, they may know nothing of the force of religion.

William James said that religion is either a dull habit or an acute fever. The dull-habit people are the formalists. The acute-fever people are those who have gotten in touch with God as a force. For them, tradition has turned into an experience, and a belief in God as the background of existence has turned into the adventure of walking with God every hour of life.

I know a man who all his life has been going to church. He has made money, lived on a materialistic plane, done the conventional things that conventional people do.

He has known that all this was not enough. He has known that his life did not match up with his professed faith. In a little group of people who had discovered the glorious adventure of faith, he saw something that made him envious so that he wanted it.

He asked questions. He prayed to God. One day when he was praying, he was telling God that he had enjoyed faith all his life, and back came the message, "Faith in yourself, but not in me."

That answer dropped the man in his tracks. It dissolved him in penitence and tears, and he surrendered himself to God as completely as he could. Since then he has been adventuring for God and with Him. He has found it not only possible but wonderful to share his new-found faith with some of his old associates. His imagination and effort are now devoted to helping others find what he has found. What was a form has become a force.

Life on your own, with God as only a background, and religion only a practice of forms—what a starved life that is! And how it is changed when living faith goes into action!

There is simply no doubt that real faith adds a power to life that was not there before. We begin finding victory over moods, depressions, and poor dispositions, through the new charge of spiritual vitality that comes through us like electricity. Spiritual vitality leads to physical vitality, so that we enjoy as great health as is possible for us. We meet the same circumstances as others—disappointment, personal loss, bewilderment, suffering—but we see them in a plan and with a purpose, not hit-or-miss and without meaning.

There is a spiritual glow that corresponds exactly with radiant good health. You know how you feel when you have gone out to walk or ride on a brisk, clear autumn day, and you come up over the crest of a hill, and the wind blows in your face, and there's a sense of almost unlimited physical well-being. I have seen this precise quality of exuberant life in the spirit of people. It makes them a joy to be with; an encouragement to everyone.

They know what it is to trust God, to listen for the whisper of His Holy Spirit, to do His will. On the human plane, this turns into a great love for people—not for just a select and congenial few, but for all who know this kind of life, and for all who need to know it.

Religion of confidence, of victory, of joy, of outgoing concern for others—that is what we all want in our heart of hearts. How do we move from form to force, from tradition to adventure?

First, we catch radiant faith from others who have it. As you can't make a fire with one stick, you can't make a spiritual fire with one life. A fire needs several, close enough to burn, with enough space between to allow for the draft to blow. The fire and the wind of the Spirit do the rest.

Second, we move from form to force if we are dissatisfied with staying as we are. A friend of mine says that if you think you are already where you want to go, you won't move! God cannot work where we refuse to move and to grow. He begins to work in our lives at the point of our dissatisfaction with our progress, or our readiness to say we need to grow and to take new ground.

Third, things happen when we look for specific blocks between ourselves and God, and root them out. When people want the comfort and power of God, they must renounce leaning on lesser things. And they must remember that real, unadmitted wrong insulates us from the power of God.

Fourth, we must step out on the promises of God. Remember: "Seek, and you will find." It is all meant for you, the abundant life which Christ promised. He did not promise that we would not have trouble; instead, He promised triumph over trouble—which is something far more glorious.

Try the experiment of prayer, of opening yourself to all of God you know or can imagine. Hand Him your problem, your perplexity, your life, and leave them with Him. Act as you feel Him leading you to act, without doubt or wavering. Let Him have that special weakness to which you cling. Take that next step of faith, about money, about doing a job, about going to work for Him.

We shall have to trust God blindly somewhere before we learn to trust Him with our eyes open. We shall have to let ourselves into positions where only faith can help us, if we are ever to find that faith is more than courage or common sense. Take God at His word, and let His promises be fulfilled in your life. Then the forms of religion will be filled with life, because we shall have found the force of religion in the power of God Himself.

Having made these general statements, let us next examine

a more specific question: How can we take a situation which we dislike, or another situation which we like all too well but which is fouling us up, and "surrender" it to God? How do we find His mind, His solution, to something thorny that really hurts?

6.

SURRENDERING A SITUATION

HERE IS A MAN, nearly forty, whose wife left him after some fifteen years of married life. He is desperately lonely, and after the first relief of having her out of the way, he finds that he misses her dreadfully and wishes they could patch things up again.

He hears an intriguing Christian message, and goes to the man who delivered it, asking for help. He begins by saying, "I suppose a person has to have a need before he can find the kind of religion you are talking about."

"Yes," the answer comes, "and would you like to say whether you have this kind of need?"

The story comes out. The man and his wife once had quite a happy life together, but as time went on, he expected her more and more to do as he wished. She became an accessory to his own life. He knew he was demanding and inconsiderate.

"Did you ever tell her you recognized this?"

No, he had not. The stubbornness of his will extended to a refusal to admit he was wrong. Now he began to see that most of the situation was of his own making, but he had neither the wisdom nor the grace to un-make it. What should he do?

There followed some talk about grace—about the living power of God coming to people and their situations. The man had been staying away from church for years, not saying his prayers except now and then to ask God to get him out of a jam.

Now his loneliness and rebellion and frustration came out in a flood of tears. Sometimes tears are like a pelting rain on a street, cleaning it completely of leaves and dirt and rubbish, and carrying them down the drain. Self-pity may be melting into penitence; it was with him.

Was he ready to put the whole situation into God's hands? Yes, he saw no other way. (Sometimes surrender comes from desperation, not yet from the drawing of God's love, except indirectly.) He had never prayed with anyone else, but this was no time to consider shyness or formalities.

"Dear God," he stammered, "help me. Show me what I ought to do. Forgive my selfishness. Bring us together again, if that's your will."

Here was no formal prayer of selfish desire; here was an honest effort to find God and His plan.

There followed a talk about loneliness, and he began to see that what he needed was not to be loved, but to learn how to love. (There simply is not enough love in the world ever to satisfy a long-hungry, selfish person. The problem is to get him over living in and for himself.)

He began to see himself in a new light. A sign of relief came into his whole expression. A new person emerged from the old shell of selfishness in which he had been encased for so long.

Some elementary helps were offered, about his own prayers, about the Church. And he was introduced to a man in his company who had just made a similar decision, so that they could meet on a new level.

Now the letter he wrote to his wife would not be a self-pitying plea that she return to a man who, in time, would do just what he had done before. Instead, it would be an honest confession of what he saw about himself, with the hope that she too might find the same dynamic faith he had begun to find, and that they might work out their situation under God's will and direction.

That man had learned to surrender his situation to God, and himself with and through the situation.

Here is another one. A man falls desperately in love with his friend's wife, and she with him. The four go on being good friends, see a lot of each other, and this love affair goes on right in the midst of what seems like the friendship of two couples.

The man is a Christian, and wants to find the Christian solution to the jam he has gotten into, involving three other people and their children. How does he surrender such a complicated situation to God?

There is a puritan and legalistic approach to this. It comes shaking a finger, saying, "This must stop. It is full of danger and sin. It must be broken off at once."

But as the man himself says, this is going to hurt several people almost beyond repair. Must he reject the woman, hurt her, refuse to see her again? This might be a safe and selfish course for his own soul, but the situation he has created has involved him in some responsibility. He may have a much more difficult thing to do than just break it off. He may have to *redeem* it.

The heavy hand of law can cause him to break off the affair as wrong, but it will take the deft hand of *grace* to change his emotions. He is told that probably he simply does not have the willpower to do it of himself, and only as God cools some of his animal heat, and changes something deep in his emotions, can there be any real solution.

There is a good long talk, and again some cleansing tears. There is no pat answer, no infallible moral rules. But it begins to appear that two things are indicated.

First, he must offer his situation to God in as full surrender as he can, taking his hands off it as completely as possible.

God has been at work already, disturbing him with guilt feelings, bringing to mind his marriage vows. But human passions are strong, and the will is weak. It is no time to shake a finger or moralize. Only understanding can help the man to face things as they must be faced.

Then comes prayer. He says, "I feel we have been sort of praying as we have been talking, with Him near us all the time." That is true. But now comes the forthright asking of God in on it, opening the doors and windows of the mind and heart to Him. And when the prayer is ended, there shines again in blurred eyes the first look of hope. He says, "This is the first time I have seen daylight in this situation."

Second, there comes the indication that he must talk this over with the woman involved, telling her what has happened and seeking to draw her into the Divine Encounter also. God always has another move to make, beginning where we are. This man has found God. The woman may find God through him. The whole situation may be redeemed because God has been allowed to come in at one corner of it.

That's the way grace works, and law has no counterpart to it. Remember how the Pharisees wanted to stone the woman taken in adultery? Jesus said, "Neither do I condemn you; go, and do not sin again" (John 8:11, RSV). They were so self-righteous in their moral zeal, and Jesus was so merciful while making the moral point clear. Which attitude redeems the person who has done wrong?

Here is another situation, apparently insoluble. A young man lives with his mother and stepfather while he is attending college. There is not much money and there is constant bickering and strife to the point that it saps him of ambition and the dynamic of creative living.

Some would leave home under such conditions, and I have known situations where it was a choice of a family's domination or God's will in a young person's life, and separation was the only solution, at whatever cost.

But this boy feels he ought to stay and see it through. How can he? Really only as he surrenders his situation to God. That is hard to do, for it involves all the hours when he is not at school.

Yes, but the old truth is still in force: there are two considerations—what happens, and how I take what happens and what I let it do to me. I cannot perhaps change the situation, but I can change my attitude toward the situation. There is such a thing as a calm at the center of a whirlwind, and there is such a thing as living in the midst of a thorny and unhappy situation with quietness and peace of heart. There will be, I suspect, times when we will lose one or both of these, but they will return when we bring the situation once more into God's hands.

So this young man is not battered and bruised by his situation—he is challenged by it, and he sees some values in it that would escape anyone who was not trying to see it from God's angle.

For instance, he sees that his present suffering (and it is real) may be his foundation for understanding other people's suffering, and he longs to help people in vital, spiritual ways. He does not enjoy his situation, but he is not overcome by it, and he sees in it some spiritual possibilities.

So he goes on getting his education and living his life in the strength of a Power not his own. Young as he is, he has learned the secret of surrendering his situation to God.

7.

BELIEVING AND DOING

THE THREE STORIES in the previous chapter describe people who learned how to surrender a situation to God, and who thus came into a deeper experience of faith and trust than they had known before. All three were, at least to some extent, "believers" at the start, and two of them were professing Christians.

What about the person to whom God is only a vague impression, and Christ merely an historical (or perhaps mythical) figure? Is there an answer, a new direction or insight for him?

Yes—provided two conditions exist. The first is that there must be a sense of *need*, as was emphasized in Chapter 2, and the second is that there must be a willingness to *experiment.*

There is an intriguing verse in St. John's gospel (chapter 7, verse 17, based on ASV): "If any man wills to do his [God's] will, he shall know of the teaching, whether it is of God, or whether I speak from myself." We might boil this down to say that Jesus implied, "Don't begin at the theological end; begin at the moral end."

The person who comes to understand the "teaching" is the person who begins by trying to square his life up with what he knows of God's will. His first impulse may be a bad conscience, an outraged sense of decency, self-disgust, or the urge to "do right."

Don't hunt up theological problems and try to answer them before you begin your spiritual search. Face the things in your own life that you know are wrong—the things you know you ought to be doing and aren't doing. Face your sins as honestly as you can.

As you begin letting the will of God take effect in your life in the places where you know it, you will learn more about what it will mean in the places where as yet you do *not* know it, and you will also understand better the theological background and foundation of the Christian faith.

Don't say, "How can I believe in such a thing as everlasting life?" Say, "What is there in my life and faith that is worth preserving forever? Am I living the kind of life that has in it hints and foretastes of eternity?"

In all experimentation, including spiritual experimentation, there is the necessity of taking the hypothesis and holding it long enough to test its validity, of "acting as if" it were true until it is proved by experience to be true or false. This is the practical approach to faith that has been literally a godsend to many people. They have said, "I don't have to begin by gulping a lot of theology I don't understand and therefore can't say I believe. I can begin by trying to square up my life a little more with the things I know God would want me to do, if there should be a God."

Nobody ever learned to swim except by acting as if he knew how to swim, and so finding out. Nobody can learn to ride a bicycle, or play tennis, or speak in public, or write a poem, until he acts as if he could do these various things. Of course he will fall off the bicycle once or twice; he may almost get drowned in the pool; but he will *learn by doing*.

Pascal saw this truth very clearly, that as we are obedient to what we know we should do, we begin to understand more about God and also more about our moral duty. He said, "If a man of goodwill expresses in practice the deeds and gestures which normally proceed from religious experience, there is opened to him a channel for the grace of God. There is thus provided a bridge between intellectual assent and the actual experience of God, supplying a continuity otherwise lacking. . . ."

Pascal also gives his corrective to those who say they would change their way of life if they only had faith. He tells them to say rather, "I should soon have faith if I were to leave my way of life."

Intellectual assent does not come first. It never did.

The truth is that some of us are so set in our ways that God never has a chance to come in and make a difference to us. Faith and understanding come only as we recognize the need for greater dedication and surrender on our part to as much as we know of God. This always involves doing something we have not been doing, and beginning to do something that we never did before.

Begin with what is wrong with your life, face and confess it, ask God to change it, and you will be surprised at how your faith clears up. It is always the "pure in heart" who see God, not the intellectually bright nor the theologically learned.

Now let us look at another verse from Scripture, also in John's gospel (chapter 6, verse 29, RSV), which provides the complement to the verse we have just explored briefly. "This is the work of God, that you believe in him whom he has sent." Jesus is saying that He is the one God has sent, and we are told to believe in Him.

We could simplify and reduce Christianity down to "acting and doing," but we would miss the most important part. God doesn't want you to follow rules; he wants your heart, your love. He also wants you to recognize what He has done in imparting Himself to the world through Jesus Christ.

What do you want from your child: punctilious obedience to what you tell him to do, or his love? The point is that if you have the love of his heart, he will want to cooperate with you even if he makes mistakes. But he can feign conformity to your wishes from fear or from wanting some reward. What matters really is what is in his heart. This truth is what enabled St. Augustine to say, "Love God and do as you please." Obviously, if you love God, the things you will be pleased to do are the things that please Him.

This is the truth so badly needed by many who believe only in that half-truth (found nowhere in the Bible): "God helps those who help themselves." That is humanism, not Christianity. Of course, it is partly true: we must cooperate with God, we must do what we know. But you will not find faith merely through wondering and thinking.

We must remember that there is nothing distinctively Christian about being honest or pure or straight in our dealings. These may be characteristics of anyone: Moslems, Jews, agnostics, even atheists.

The distinctive thing in Christianity is always our faith in Jesus Christ. It is true, as St. James says, that 'faith without works is dead,' but it is also true that works without faith are dead. Good deeds, right deeds, loving deeds flow from faith, but they are never a substitute for faith.

The question then comes: Where do we get our "light"? How are we going to know, finally, what we should do? Where will we find the spiritual help that gives us the incentive to do God's will, and where will we find forgiveness when we miss it and disobey?

I find great comfort and strength in this verse: "This is the work of God, that you believe in him whom he has sent" (John 6:29, RSV). The first obligation for a Christian lies in his faith in his Lord and Saviour. Moral living stems from that.

But the great and final thing is the "teaching"—the whole of it: Christ's teaching about Himself, who He is as the Son of God and the Saviour of the world; His teaching about God and His love for the world; His teaching about man and life and our eternal destiny.

This is not primarily ethical teaching about how we should behave, though it includes this. It is teaching that gives life its meaning and framework, that sets our lives in the context of the divine plan, and the revelation of that plan in Jesus Christ.

It surely cannot mean that we have nothing to do but find a satisfactory faith and continue to believe in it for ourselves. This is, rather, the universal truth about life, for all people at all times and in all places. To discover it is like discovering a cure for cancer: we cannot possibly accept it just for ourselves, we must spread it wherever there is need.

No other spiritual leader in history made the claims for himself that our Lord made, nor accepted the incredible words of personal homage that His disciples gave Him. When you touch Him, you touch something like radium at the center of history. When you put your trust in Him, you know beyond any doubt that He holds the secret to life.

Increasingly we are led into the great mysteries of the Cross and the Resurrection, one dealing with the sin of man, and the other with victory over death itself. In the wake of Christ's faith has followed most of the humanitarian good that has been done these twenty centuries, and more of it needs doing now than ever. Do you see why Jesus Christ could call it "the work of God" to believe in Him? Once the faith is ours, this kind of work follows.

So there is an obedience that must precede true understanding faith. And then there is a deep faith that must send us back again into the world empowered to live out His will. This is the inspired cycle of believing and doing.

Does your experimental nature extend to these two spiritual tests? First, bring your life into line with God's will as you understand or infer it. Second, get to know Jesus Christ, through other people and through reading what He said about Himself and what others said about Him.

For this latter experiment, set aside some time each day

when you can be quiet and alone, and get hold of a good modern translation of the New Testament (Moffatt's, J. B. Phillips', or *The New English Bible*), which you may want to compare with the majestic cadences of the King James Version.

Who knows—you may find windows opening, fresh air coming in, and new light shining through!

8.

GROWING UP SPIRITUALLY

NO MATTER AT WHAT POINT we may be in the adventure of life, I don't think any of us should be satisfied with our spiritual progress and growth. Let's think, then, about spiritual immaturities, and see what we can do to overcome them, and to "grow up into Christ," as St. Paul urges us to do.

One of the commonest occasions for an exhibition of spiritual childishness is when trouble comes. How often our faith gives way! Either we say God has failed us, or we take a position that says, "Why did God do this to me? I have always tried to do what is right."

Here we show that we have not grown up enough to realize that our faith is not intended to save us from *trouble*, but from *defeat*. How can we grow petulant and think God is showing spite or injustice, when we share the universal tribulations which come upon all men at some time or in some way? Our attitude shows that we have never really gotten down to what faith is and what it is for.

Another way in which we show spiritual immaturity is in the way we react to the mistakes of others. Most of us are very tolerant of our own shortcomings and mistakes, and very critical of other people's. We ought to know by now that the Church is not a museum, but a hospital—not a showcase, but a school.

Still another childish behavior is to take color from the

paganism about us. Paganism makes a dent on us in two ways: (1) by drawing us on to chime in with some skeptical, even atheistic point of view, when we do not know and believe enough to make a decent defense; and (2) by making us feel we have to be "good Joes" and do just what people do who make no religious profession.

A half-baked youngster hears some skeptical remarks in a college classroom, or gets into a dormitory discussion where religion is being panned, and he concludes he must be an atheist! Or our immaturity shows if we take offense and behave as if people were speaking about us personally. But surely we ought to be old enough and have enough convictions to make a good-natured and telling defense of our faith.

Spiritual immaturity is evident, also, when we throw our weight around in the family or at work. A man has never quite grown up, so he becomes the family tyrant who wants to bend everyone to his will. Or the head of the company is still a little boy who loves to get satisfaction by thundering his orders.

Equal immaturity is evinced, I am sure, in those who do not stand up to these parlor and office dictators. It is not being a great Christian, but a spineless doormat, to let somebody get away with this kind of thing. Justice may have to be the forerunner of love, where love has been lost or where it never existed.

One more kind of immaturity is the childish faith that would "use" God. The mature motive in religion is always to glorify God, rather than ourselves by the use we make of God. Of course, in a sense, we are always children before Him, but when shall we quit trying to get God to do our will, and begin trying to find His will?

Lee Bristol, Jr., says that there are Christians "in order that" and Christians "because of." The "in order that" people try to bend God to their will. The "because of" people live from gratitude for what God has done for them.

Let us look at some of the things which keep us from growing up spiritually.

The first, I am sure, is a satisfied feeling that we are in the process of growing, when actually we are only in the process of hardening by custom. We do not like to think about the deep dissatisfaction which must precede real growth. Some of us are not Christians, we are just wearing a religious mask or doing a religious job.

Second, we fear to be different from the crowd. We are right not to want to be oddities and fanatics, but that is not our chief danger! There is a dreadful conformity, a dead-level kind of mediocrity all around us today, and we take our cue much more from it than from Christ.

Third, we may never have decisively begun a Christian life at all. You can rub your arm with a scalpel, and produce an abrasion that will admit a vaccine. Or, you can rub it less strenuously, and produce a callous. Some of us need a vaccination—or a great, overall Christian decision.

The fourth thing that keeps us from growing is the deception of perfectionism. It is right to take so absolute a model as Christ, but it is sure that we cannot "grow up in all things into Him" in a hurry. Von Hugel spoke of "the mysterious yet very certain truth that we can actually hamper our advance by trying too directly, too vehemently, too much by absolute recipes or models. . . ." And Fenelon said, "It is an excess of self-love that would become perfect in a moment, rather than by slow degrees." Seeking quick perfection, we fail and become discouraged, and give up.

Let us now consider some of the ways in which we grow toward spiritual maturity.

We grow spiritually by having to make decisions. Decisions, even wrong ones, are ways to grow by, and nobody meets life without making them. Look the facts in the face, take wise human counsel, lay the situation before God in prayer, and decide as you think He wants you to. Right choices added together are right character and right direction. We need thought and we need prayer, but moony mysticism makes people avoid life, not meet it.

We grow also as we give ourselves lavishly to other people. Sometimes we need to forget our own growth in favor of somebody else. In his magazine, *Democracy in Action*, Melvin Evans says,

> We grow as we become interested in the other fellow, and develop sincere, unselfish enthusiasm for him, willingness to identify ourselves with him in his difficulties. As we achieve a warm, close sense of comradeship, we are able to put our shoulder to the wheel and help him out of his rut. The magic of it all is that in so doing we climb out of our own seemingly insurmountable difficulty. We grow by trouble.

We ought to be artists in turning evil into good, finding how God can transform what looks like sheer waste, or tragedy, or wrong, into an occasion for His ingenious love to go to work, perhaps through us.

We grow as we learn what St. Paul meant by "speaking the truth in love." Many times we speak the truth in anger or domination or self-justification. And sometimes when we are loving, we only seem loving, for actually we are hiding the truth we feel, mistaking cowardice and sentimentality for love.

I say without hesitation that people who can get across the truth to others without becoming unloving, those who can keep a real, human relationship while they are dealing with acute and unpleasant factors, are the most mature people in the world. Plenty of us are sentimental, which leaves out the truth; and many of us are blunt, which leaves out the love.

We grow as we learn more and more that the Christian

faith is the one thing that solves life, and as we get into the stream of it. I think this means having had such a steady and increasing experience of Christ that some knotty problem, some eloquent skeptic, some knockdown blow will not unseat our faith. Knowing doctrine is good: knowing Him whom the doctrine concerns is better.

And finally we grow as we keep opening ourselves to new challenges. It is easy to say, especially as we grow older, "This is the kind of person I am, and it's too late to change." This is heresy—virtual atheism. If we go to church to be lulled by sweet music and soft words, if long ago we accepted ourselves and have no real intention of changing, if we just settle for a little "peace," we shall never let ourselves "grow up into Him."

Arnold Toynbee says that more than half of Egyptian history is a "gigantic epilogue." Centuries ago Egypt stopped growing. Is our life more than half epilogue? Is it the suffix and aftermath of a life that once was growing, but has now stopped?

9.

LET MORE COME THROUGH!

DO YOU SOMETIMES FEEL that you are not living at one half or even one tenth of your real potential? Maybe you are not making the most of your opportunities, or maybe you have a friend who is in great need whom you would like to help, but the power just isn't there.

Sometimes when you are watering the garden, the flow suddenly stops. When you look to see what is the matter, you find not that someone has turned off the water, but that the hose has twisted on itself and caused a constriction, so that the water does not come through freely.

We all know people who are like this. Nothing seems to be flowing into them from outside, with renewal and fresh inspiration. They are unfortunate, locked-up people, not living to a fraction of their capacity. When someone else is in trouble, their hearts are touched and they wish they could "do something," but their inner lives are dry and empty, their imagination is small, and they are so little in touch with any source of inspiration that they are tongue-tied.

And we know people who are just the opposite. Their emotions seem free. They enjoy life and other people. When disappointment or trouble come to them, they have a reservoir on which to draw. When they meet another person in trouble, they radiate concern, goodwill, and sympathy, so that at once the person in trouble begins to draw on them, as if he were thirsty and had been handed a glass of water.

I have such a person in mind now. He is a hard-working man who lives with his family in a small house. Outwardly there is nothing that suggests wealth. The surroundings could be duplicated ten million times. But inwardly and spiritually you find wealth—wealth of love and understanding and joy.

His wife and children are deeply loved and enjoyed. There is a small salary, but never a sense of poverty. When he joins a group of people anywhere, he comes in quietly and smiling. He is soon talking with others about the things that interest them, finding out about them, giving himself to them.

I think he is always praying with the back of his mind to be a channel, while listening interestedly with the front of his mind. He leaves you with the feeling that you matter to him, and that contact with him has put a spiritual deposit in your heart and spirit.

Let us say that you are trying to help someone in desperate trouble, pain, grave illness. You don't know much theology or psychology, and you don't want to say something that will only make matters worse. If you are honest, you know that there is not much more you can do than to express your sympathy and show your concern.

These are not enough, of course, but better these alone than something forced, "gushy," unreal. What you really want is some deep release way down inside your own emotions that helps you feel more as the person you want to help is feeling, and enables you to come to closer grips with the situation. You must throw yourself on the mercy and grace of a Power greater than yourself, asking for guidance as to how you can be maturely helpful.

A trained nurse was alone with a patient who was suffering terribly and cursing God for his pain. In her own strength, all the nurse could do was to give him the prescribed medication, which evidently was not doing him very much good.

She believed in Christ, and she believed in prayer, so she began silently "lifting up" the patient and commending him to God. There is prayer that is little more than spoken desperation, and there is prayer that is so believing that God uses it as an avenue of release toward its object. The nurse prayed in the latter way.

The man fell off to sleep and slept all through the night, while she kept "praying at" his subconscious self. Next morning he awakened, his pain gone, saying that in some unaccountable way he found himself loving God for the first time in his life!

Thoreau said that most men live lives of quiet desperation. I think that is true. Rascals may try to cut their way out of that prison of boredom, but it is apt to get them into other kinds of trouble. But for sheer, prosaic dullness, the lives of many "good" people take the prize. It is a miracle when a very bad person gets converted into a very good one. It is even more of a miracle when people for whom life is dull and lackluster find such an experience of God that life gets exciting for them.

Not long ago I spent a thrilling half-hour with such a man. Some long-ago incident had cast a shadow over his family, and he lived in a self-imposed darkness. Then he moved into a new neighborhood, and he and his family came into contact with a dynamic Christian faith. They heard that no one needs to live under such a shadow. If there is guilt, ask God for forgiveness and accept it, and go forward. If there is fear or shame, ask God to release it, and then accept His help.

One evening the man and his wife decided to hand their lifelong problem over to God. They prayed, they surrendered it to Him verbally—and it went! They came out into the daylight.

Since then, they have touched many by their own adventurous lives. They have had some difficult financial problems to deal with, but a solution always seems to come. At the time we talked, the man was paying off old debts and getting squared away for the future. But the thrilling thing about him is the joy and wonder in his life at God's ways and provision.

People who live in the mainstream of faith have a dimension in their lives that most others know nothing of. It is not a matter of tugging at your own bootstraps. It is something that comes through to you. Effort gives place to obedience, apprehension to faith, boredom to the wonder of life.

This man and his wife were once stricken people, knowing little of any outside Power, and letting almost nothing through. Today their lives are "charged" with the power of God.

I know a young couple who have not had easy sledding in their married life. They have faced many problems, inside and outside the relationship. The wife had a real faith, and the husband a pretty good inkling of it. They started to pray together, and to go to church with regularity. But not until two and a half years had passed did it become natural and easy for them to pray. It took that long for prayer's effects to get way down into their emotions.

Conventional religion never thawed their tensions, but when they began to "let more through," to be released and expectant, things began to happen. Now they are at work trying to keep another couple from divorce. Out of their own experience, they know what Christ can do. They are not bottling this up in pride and selfish hoarding; they are giving to the other couple what has come to them.

Everywhere, it seems to me, in the desperate physical needs of the underprivileged people of the world for life's common necessities, in the dry and loveless efforts to work out better relations between tense groups in our own country, and in the hearts of people about us who are starved for love, there is a cry for something which can never be answered unless we let God first give us a great emotional release through a great openness to Him.

Did you ever look down an old-fashioned well and wonder where the water came from? Year after year water is drawn out, and year after year there is always more. There is no direct pipe which fills it. No—the water seems to seep in from all sides, in tiny rivulets of steady flow.

Just so does the love and mercy and buoyancy and sufficiency of God flood in upon us from all sides, when we let it happen, filling up the drained resources of our human sympathies, emotions, and energies.

Let us look not so much for health-builders, not for psychological formulas to encourage ourselves. Let us rather throw open the deep places of our lives to the light and love of God. Let us expose the hurt places—the tired places—the dry places—the hopeless places—the loveless places—the places of fear and bewilderment and frustration—and let the powers of what Masefield called "The Everlasting Mercy" take over.

Let us not struggle more, but accept more. Let us not try more, but trust more. Let us not drive ourselves more, but draw more upon God. Let us let more come through—and life will be a thousand times richer, for us and for all those about us.

II. Living Is EXCHANGE

10.

A FIVE-POINT PLAN

THERE ARE PROBABLY countless thousands of people who would honestly like to live a Christian life, but have never been told how to do it. They believe that faith helps people to live, and that Christian ideals are most likely right. They sense that there is a "Higher Power" in the universe and they long for some touch with that Power. They alternate between a preoccupation with the things of this world, and an aspiration after the things of the spirit.

Doesn't that describe many people you know? Are you, perhaps, one of those people? It is not so much an argument to prove the truth of religion that you want, but someone to tell you *how* to make faith work in ordinary life.

Here is a five-point plan for living which can be followed by anyone who is willing to give it a try. Some of the points have already been discussed in preceding chapters, but they bear repeating.

* * *

The first point is *the need for a changed heart.* The longer we think about God and pray to Him, the clearer it becomes that religion does not mean our using God for our own ends, but letting God use us for His ends. Religion begins when we accept the fact that God's will is the primary objective of every believer, and that everything in us which is outside God's will is sin. That is to say, religion begins for us when we surrender ourselves to God.

Sometimes we little understand ourselves and we need to go talk with someone who is spiritually further along than we, in a conversation in which we can be frank about our lives. Surrender has little content unless it involves the giving up of whatever stands between us and God. The sins of passion will occur to us first, and then the sins of attitude, which are subtler and may be more devastating.

Of course we do not convert ourselves; God's Holy Spirit alone can change a man's heart. But God is ready to transform us if we will give in to Him. Conversion is only a beginning. We need nourishment, growth, and training. There is an additional decision—and then a lifetime of discipleship. But one has to begin, and the changed heart is the doorway into the Christian life.

2. The second point is *the need for daily contact with God in private devotions.* When we are born into the new life, we need sustenance. The Bible, along with other books to help us understand the Christian life, provides our "food."

If the Bible is our food, prayer is our "air." It is the way by which we draw in the atmosphere of God. Prayer is rich and varied. Sometimes we confess our sins in a prayer of penitence. Sometimes we praise God in worship and thanksgiving. Sometimes we ask God for help and grace to meet whatever comes our way. Sometimes we pray for other people. Sometimes we are quiet, knowing that when we stop clamoring and pleading our case, there comes a sense of God's reply, some intimation of His will, some message from Him to us. Remember that nothing God can ever give is comparable to *Himself*. It is *God* we seek in prayer; everything else is secondary.

It is our experience that the continuation of the Christian life depends primarily upon the regularity and fidelity with which we work out and pursue our daily devotional life. Keep at it until you find your way. Change the pattern a bit when it grows stale. But do it every day, no matter what else goes undone.

Not long ago I saw a friend who only a few months back seemed soft, indulgent, and lacking in spiritual power. Now his life was crisp—it crackled with the supernatural. He was obviously in touch with God, and God was working in him and through him. What had happened? That man was getting up every morning at 6:30 and spending the first hour of his day in Bible study, prayer, and meditation. He had found the secret.

The third point is *our need for fellowship.* Christianity is not only believing in the things Jesus taught but belonging to the movement He started. The early Church was not a set of separate individuals who believed in Christ; it was a lot of people bound together in the fellowship of His Church.

The Church has never ceased. We can still belong to it, and must, if we are going to follow Him. Think what we miss if we want to "eat the morsel alone," and try to live solo when fundamental Christianity is inherently and organically corporate!

Within the larger fellowship of the Church, we need smaller groups or "cells"—Christians who come together regularly to pray, study, and possibly work out common projects. Here we come to be known and to know others. Our problems can come into the open. We can tell about our victories and express our needs.

You can't organize fellowship. One who "leads" such a group must be careful to let Christ lead it through him. If all are listeners, then all can be leaders. No raised voices, no place for declaiming or pontificating. Everyone's mind and heart turned upward toward God, outward toward each other. And then what power, what light, what joy, what stimulus to new living, faith, health, and readiness to meet anything that may come!

The fourth point is *the need to work all this out in our homes, our human relationships, and in the places where we work.* If our hearts are changed, the family will know it first. Beyond anything we can say, they will see that God has subdued that bad temper, hastiness, fear, negativeness, or whatever has made us unconvincing in the past.

When we fail, let us admit it honestly, and not justify ourselves for falling down. As it works out, let us include others in the family in praying with us, and seeking God's plan for them and for the household. As the children see that we look to a Higher Authority than ourselves, they will find that they can look to Him also, and that as we all meet in Him, we can find unity together.

Christ gives us a whole new concept of human relationships. It is dynamic, not static. Nine tenths of the evil in the world in this appalling day goes back to strained, dishonest, broken human relationships. If you are in touch with God, He can work through you to come into a situation with love, with honesty, by getting to the root of division, and by bringing cooperation and trust and faith.

Fear holds many of us from daring to live out our faith at work; our personal religion is one thing, our business quite another. But business and politics are the body of our common, daily life. They are full of corruption because men will not dare to stand by their principles—losing office, losing money if necessary rather than compromising, but demonstrating something through loss (as Christ did on the cross), and creating a stepping-stone to a "success" which is more real. If Christianity does not work in your job, it does not work at all.

The fifth point is *our privilege and obligation to help other people.* Christianity did not begin with a few professionals organizing a publicity campaign and holding mass meetings. It began with one man telling another about Christ, and what Christ had done in his own life.

The method of basic Christianity has not changed, for human nature remains the same and Christ does not change. Everyone has a problem, a need, a fear—and that is probably the place at which he will find Christ.

People need someone to tell them how they can conquer that fear, meet that need, solve that problem. You can't do it with good ideas, but only with your own and others' experiences. We must help people to face the sins that underlie the problem. Above all, they must see in us a faith, a joy, an assurance that Christ has the answer to every human need. They will want Him, seek Him, find Him, give themselves to Him.

And what of the larger issues today? Do they need anything so much as Christian character and Christian community—individual men and women with the integrity most of the world lacks, and the power to live and work together for want of which the world is committing suicide? Character and community are the raw material of the only kind of new world I want to live in. If you feel that way, let us all get together and live out the great elementals we have sought to set down in this five-point plan. A growing minority of people living that way can change the course of history.

11.

DON'T BE AFRAID!

WE ALL KNOW how prevalent fear is. Sometimes we fear people, sometimes we fear the future, sometimes we fear fear itself. Sometimes our fears are vague and nebulous, yet sufficient to cause us misery. Even for those of us who are attempting to live in the stream of God's life, fear is unsettling. It may make us turn in on ourselves, and it may destroy our ability to help others.

For this reason, one of the most wonderful and welcome things Jesus ever said was, "Fear not." He always perceived what was in the human heart, and He knew how often fear overruled everything else.

Don't think, however, that Jesus taught that there is nothing to fear. The great chapter on fear is Luke 12. He tells us there what not to fear, but He also tells us what we should fear. One thing to fear is hypocrisy and spiritual faking (and He says that everything hidden will in the end be revealed).

Jesus believed in the power of God. He wanted everybody to know it and respond to it. He wanted people to realize the eternal consequences of ignoring it, too. He warns us solemnly to fear those consequences. We all know that it is well to teach children to be afraid of an open window or a swift-moving car, or being careless in a real sickness. There would not be fear in the world, as there would not be opium, unless there were some use for it.

Yet the total impact of Jesus, while reminding us of rightful fears, is to help dispel the needless and destructive fears with which our lives are often filled.

Let us think of some of the things that He would like to dispel from our minds. I believe He would say something like this:

Don't be afraid of doubt! Faith is something which comes to people who look facts in the face, including the greatest fact of all, the fact of God. Most of us do believe. But as there is greater strength in a steel bridge that sways a bit in the wind than in one made absolutely rigid, so there is more strength to a faith that now and then shares the emotion of doubt. Not, mind you, doubt as a fixed and settled attitude—that is negative and destructive—but rather an inclusive feeling that only the man who has dared to doubt has the right to believe, and that God (if He is God) will overcome our doubts by revealing more and more of Himself.

There may be points of faith which we do not yet accept: let us not swallow them simply "on authority," but seek to work them out with our minds plus God's inspiration. There is the mood of doubt that may be caused by indigestion or a bad liver, and there is the mood of doubt that sweeps us now and then when evil presses hard. Faith does not dispel doubt by making us fear to admit or face it; faith dispels doubt by winning out over it in an honest duel.

Don't be afraid of evil! I mean not only the personal evil that attacks us with temptation, or disaster, or suffering; I mean great, general evil, always threatening us with meaninglessness or annihilation. In some places and situations one can feel evil as a positive force. I have been in cities where this was true, and with people or groups of people where I felt it. But God has a strange way of using evil and making it serve His ends in the long run. We depend on a kind of ingenuity in God, as well as on His innate goodness.

Don't be afraid of pain! All of us have known pain in sharp twinges, some of us in long, unrelieved stretches. Just why it is here we cannot say, but we do know that many have won their finest victories over it, and have found in it a peace greater than the pain.

I knew well one of the first experimenters with X-ray. He had burned his hands terribly and had lost most of his right hand. The pain of his skin cancer was devastating and in his later years so severe that, giant as he was, the tears would stream down his face.

But his need drove him back to a God he had lost. He experienced a wonderful partial healing and died in the fullness of faith. He told me that he and pain had been "pretty close companions" for a number of years, and that he had learned how to overcome the fear of it. He helped to show me what wonderful triumphs can come out of what seem unrelieved tragedies.

Don't be afraid of trouble! We all tend to look for happiness—but those who look for happiness never find it, while those who seek to get into the stream of God's life and will and power, and who do what He wants of them, seem to come by happiness almost unawares.

We are sometimes dashed by disappointment—in our fondest hopes, in people we trusted, through failure or what looks like failure. Many people will say that they never lived until they struck something they could not handle, and it turned them back to God! We never need be overcome by trouble. Whatever the circumstance, we can meet it in God's strength, and He can show us how to handle it.

Don't be afraid of old age! Lively and vitally interested people find it hard to hear what Dr. Hugh Black once called "the sound of closing doors about them." We cannot do what we once did. We feel weakness and even pain in the body that once knew only the joy of motion and action.

It is all very well for philosophers (especially young ones) to talk, but this is no joke for anyone.

How we meet old age depends really on how much faith we have let God give us. An elderly friend of mine, with almost no money and a broken back, seldom stirring from her room, wrote of what she thought was cowardice on the part of some younger people:

> If old people don't go along with the times they can't expect us youngsters to dally along with them. . . . I feel like new wine in an old bottle. . . . It's wonderful to be living alone so I can spend my whole time reading and studying and writing, and having a broken back so no one expects me to call on them. Thank God for His blessings!

How's that for victory in old age? But the book she reads most constantly is the Bible, and the friend who keeps her company is the Great Friend, and the purpose that keeps her vitally interested in life is the will of God in the world.

Finally, don't be afraid of death! Death is a part of life itself; it is in the nature of things, it is not an intruder. None of us knows his own hour, and all of us may be living closer to death than we think. Bombs make mass-murder entirely possible. If our imaginations are vivid, we can picture some terrible scenes.

But if we have faith, I think we remember two things: (1) Man's freedom is what makes him man, and freedom means the choice is always ours between God's ways and our own. When we take our own way and not His we bring suffering, even destruction, on ourselves. (2) We "fear not them that kill the body." And our Lord adds a wonderful phrase: "and after that have no more that they can do." It makes us think of that tremendous statement in the Acts of the Apostles about the impotence of death over Christ: "It was not possible that He should be holden of it." Death having claimed His human body, its power was spent.

Jesus' resurrection was the vindication of His faith. This

faith He communicates to us. God in Christ has overcome death, and there is nothing to fear.

We do not have a faith which tells us to look to one side of life's pain and trials and hardships, which pretends that evil is not evil, that suffering is illusion, that death is not death. We have a faith which looks all these things squarely in the face and knows that God is greater than any one of them. The reason we need have no fear about either life or death is not that God exempts believing people from the trouble that comes to others. He does not. We do not fear because God never faces us with any situation He knows we cannot meet in His strength. "This is the victory that overcomes the world, even our faith."

And so comes the clear, steady voice of Christ across the centuries as if He were speaking to each of us personally, and to our condition: "Fear not!"

12.

BEING OF SOUND MIND . . .

WHATEVER LIFE WAS MEANT TO BE, it evidently was not meant to be easy. The world may be a boudoir in which to seek as many pleasant sensations as we can find, or it may be a battlefield where real issues are being worked out, but it certainly is not a limousine in which we are whisked along forever in comfortable irresponsibility. Life is a problem.

Where does life come from? Where is it going? Why is the burden of it laid upon us at all? Almost every healthy, independent spirit has at times felt a kind of rebellion against God or fate for putting him in this world at all. We are torn between desire and duty, between the thing that our instincts and emotions cry for, and the thing which our reason and our conscience demand. What are we going to do?

Having concluded that there are things from which we are not to cringe in abject fear, let us take a somewhat deeper look at some of these thorny problems of our existence.

Once more comes the question of evil—especially suffering and sin. Suffering comes in differing ways to all, without regard to their virtue. Sin seems more mysterious still. It is no good to say that there are also much pleasure and goodness in the world—these do not cancel or explain away evil.

And then at the other end of the road stands death. No, we are not to fear it, but as Gamaliel Bradford says, "We all see death before us, with its plunge into the gulf of the utterly unknown, and however we may laugh or trifle, or endeavor to forget, or rush hither and thither in agitated fury, the dread of death has a quiet, cold, nestling corner in the heart of every one of us."

Here we are, bracketed between a riddle and a pit, and stung every day by the mystery of trouble and sorrow. No theory about life is worth considering which does not face these problems in their stark reality.

And these considerations have brought about certain secondary problems, which are perhaps especially present in our time.

The first, again, is fear. A great, elementary fear about the worthwhileness of life itself mothers a brood of little fears. Psychiatrists' offices and Christian Science experience meetings are full of people seeking an escape from fear.

Another fruit of uncertainty is restlessness. We live in a land and in an age where mechanical devices have been developed with breath-taking rapidity, while ethical and spiritual development has stood still or gone backward. The things which make life look like a complicated trap proliferate every day—and the things that give sense and reason and significance to life are at a discount.

We have been told to substitute the esthetic for the philosophical and the religious—to make our lives beautiful so that we need not bother about these high considerations. In other words, paint your trap sky blue, and plant some flowers in it, and it will not seem so much like a trap! This is the last refuge of sentimentality.

Still another problem is that of emotional instability. One of the psychologists in a great state institution told me that in nearly half of the patients who come to him, the cause of the breakdown is not paresis or brain deterioration from old age, illness, or alcoholism. The patients have simply lost their grip on and confidence in life. They are unable to cope with life in a self-supporting and happy fashion, and have either sought refuge in the hospital or been taken there by their families.

There is a fourth group whose problem grows out of maladaptation to life: those with an inferiority complex. A severe maladjustment results in a sense of isolation from the rest of humanity. In other cases, it ranges all the way from complete frustration and inability to meet life, to a vague feeling of being ill at ease with those considered superior.

In the scuffle and competition of modern life, such mental disorders have increased, and the proper adjustment of the individual remains a prime concern of human civilization. But there is a place where science stops. A psychiatrist said to a member of my staff, "Psychiatry has learned to make an accurate diagnosis and to recommend a useful plan, but psychiatry cannot furnish the motive which will make the patient want to *follow* the plan."

I believe that Jesus Christ is needed for the completeness of mental health. If maladjustment to one's environment is to be cured, one must finally be put into relationship with his *whole* environment—not just his family or village, or what is vaguely called "society," but also with the cosmos. Jesus Christ speaks for the universe and represents it; by word and act He declares it friendly and meaningful. As a matter of plain, demonstrable experience, men do come into correspondence and harmony with the universe through Him. The extraordinary contribution of the religion of Christ to mental health begins in giving to human beings a sense of security and safety in the universe itself.

Christianity has never given a pat theoretical solution to the question of evil. In the pages of the Bible you will find ways to deal with evil, but very little philosophy about where it comes from or why it is present. But Christianity does assure us that God is not indifferent to our struggle with evil, nor does He stand aloof from it. He came down into it (that is the religion of the incarnation) and dealt with it (that is the religion of the cross and the atonement).

Jesus was taken to the cross by a lot of cautious, jealous ecclesiastics, and by an utterly indifferent government. Thus considered, it was an unmitigated tragedy. But Jesus made something else of the cross—a willing and voluntary sacrifice which He took upon Himself "for us men and for our salvation."

The cross transfigures suffering. God does not send evil upon us, I am sure, but when we take our trouble as Christ took His cross, it is transformed and finds a meaning.

We all know Jesus' belief about death: that it is a gateway into life beyond. Materialists say that Christians have invented immortality as a protest against their own insignificance, and as a sop to their desire not to be extinguished.

I do not deny the difficulty of believing in immortality, but the craving for immortality is almost universal. Jesus has been found right where we can follow Him in experience, and I for one am willing to believe Him when He speaks of that which I cannot discover now, but shall know hereafter.

If Christianity is true, we are not like animals in a trap, but rather like children in a home. We are not bracketed between a riddle and a pit, but between an adventure and a vision of God. Trouble and pain are part of the adventure.

As for the lesser things, Christianity does not take the restlessness out of a man; it transfers its direction. Restlessness need not be peevish and personal, but unselfish and magnificent, spurring us on to making a new world. Discomfort and insecurity are lost in the great struggle.

As for fear, perfect love casts out fear. Trumping up false confidence and courage is no cure—but faith is. The more you trust God, the more sure you will be that He can be trusted.

Similarly with emotional lack of control. When do we break down, sink into depression, fly into hysterics? Is it not when the bottom has dropped out—when men cannot be trusted and God is gone? But the bottom need not drop out for the Christian. He often loses faith in himself—but that only drives him back to Christ. When a man has God, he has everything.

As for inferiority, religion is the only true and permanent cure. Religion begins with our own inferiority to God. Let a man get *that* adjustment clear in his mind, and the rest of our high or low thoughts about ourselves fall into line. Let a man submit himself to God, who deserves submission, and he will stand on his own two feet with his fellows.

There is no more merciful fact in this world than that health is as contagious as sickness—especially mental health. What do you suppose it does to the interior life of a harassed and nervous and fearful person to keep thinking about Jesus Christ—thinking of His buoyancy, His radiance and cheerfulness, His sanity and common sense, His infinite hope for us and faith in us—that we can be different, that we can win out, that we can have His abundance of life?

Here indeed is a spur toward confident, hopeful, and resplendent living! But our debt to Him, the derivative quality of our life, makes us always conscious that we have not gotten this victory ourselves, and keeps us from egotism and self-centeredness.

All this implies a relationship to Christ. It is not a borrowed outlook or ethic which comes from Him, but it is He Himself who gives this health. "Acquaint now thyself with him" —not with His philosophy, nor with His world view, nor with His theology, but with Him personally—"and be at peace." This is no blind, dishonest evasion of life, no refuge for the distracted mind. This is an experiment open to any man or woman who will look life fair in the face, and try life with Christ as he has tried it without Him.

13.

SOMETHING NEW IS NEEDED

WHAT WOULD JESUS SAY about our churches today, and about us who speak His Name and profess to stand for Him? There are certainly a lot of us. We have fine buildings and plants, sincere and hard-working clergy, loyal and devoted people.

But if He asked whether we love God as much as we love ourselves, our businesses and daily occupations, it might be embarrassing. With the amount of time and money and life invested in our churches, do we even begin to have the effect upon a great, industrial society that we ought to have?

I am sure Jesus would be glad for what is being done, and I am sure He would not think it is enough. It has been said of Him that He is "easy to please but hard to satisfy."

As for myself, I have a deep conviction that the Church needs something else besides what it is now doing and offering to people. The amount of our spiritual "intake" far exceeds the amount of our spiritual "outgo."

Roman Catholic churches offer a constant supply of sacraments, with enough grace in them to change the world, but how great is their effect? Protestant churches offer preaching, sometimes three times a week, more than anyone can possibly take in, so that it seems to me like trying to stuff still more meat into an already overstuffed sausage skin; but nobody stops to ask what all this is doing and accomplishing in the world. My own (Episcopal) church believes both in sacraments and in preaching, but how often does our liturgy lull us into spiritual stupor, and give just enough religion to keep us fairly satisfied, but not enough to overflow in a dynamic way into the life about us?

Is the whole thing gauged to our personal wants, or is it gauged to the needs of the city, the nation, our society? Have the churches even suggested that we have a responsibility beyond our immediate wants or the functioning of our local parishes? Have they taken this responsibility seriously enough to give any sustained training to laymen?

Most of what is called "laymen's work" is nothing but drawing people into the technical work of maintaining a local congregation, looking after its finances, its plant, its operation. These things are important, but they are important only if the church is sending sound and Christian laymen out into the fields of daily life in the world to transform that daily life and bring it more into conformity to the will of Christ.

If all that happens in church is that you and I come back empty for a refill every Sunday, we are pouring water down a rat hole. Christians are not meant to be perennial babies to be fed and coddled; they are meant to be soldiers and operators for God in a world that was never more in danger of going down the road of materialism, godlessness, and revolution. The vast majority of our church people are inarticulate. Communists would reject, root and branch, as unworthy of membership in the party, people so unsure and so incompetent.

What, specifically, does the Church need—the whole Church, all churches?

First, we need a deeper experience of Jesus Christ. In our services we say many true words, but these often remain concepts only. The Church is bloated with concepts. God didn't send us a concept, He sent us a Baby! He sent a life which would produce more lives by radiation.

Faith is different from belief. You *can't* witness convincingly about the Apostles' Creed. You *can* witness about what Jesus Christ has done for you and for other people. The weakness of the Church is the telling of unembodied truth. Truth must be clothed with experience, as skeletons must be clothed with flesh and blood.

Christians ought to be engaged in a serious and determined effort to turn individual people to Christ in faith and surrender, otherwise their conversion is not likely to occur. And if genuine conversions do not occur, the stream of Christian faith and life in the world will grow thinner, turning into nothing more than a multiplicity of church members.

Thinner faith.

2. Second, we need an entirely different kind of meeting from those we have. We meet to worship, to transact business, to instruct. But we need a meeting whose whole purpose is catching the imagination of outsiders, and training insiders to do it.

Many children grow up with no religious instruction at all, and many older people have a brand of religion that would not attract an intelligent pagan. Coming to a church service may leave him mystified. He might see little relevance in a formal service to life in a hard, competitive, bewildered world.

What the Church needs most of all is small, informal gatherings, not where some professional gives you the "straight" on something, but where amateurs and experimenters tell you what they are doing to find reality in faith and life. We clergy should be much more adept in this than in preaching sermons.

Dr. Abraham Vereide is one of the great Christian leaders of our time. His daughter says, "Dad's highlight is not in a great cathedral, but around the table." We might say, so was Jesus Christ's. Every church should consider how people who would like to find a credible, relevant faith might do so in such small groups—some for beginners, some for more mature training.

I am convinced, also, that meetings like this can well be of an interdenominational character. There is a Christianity that is basic to Presbyterians, Methodists, Episcopalians, Roman Catholics, Pentecostals, and Quakers. Keep to Christ and off denominational differences. Keep to what has happened.

A group like this has in mind from the first not only the cultivation of real personal faith in the life of each individual, but also the relating of all this to the problems of the city, of the nation, of the world.

Professor Alfred C. Ackenheil, of the University of Pittsburgh, says, "The cell group is the way to get and dispense information on God and country." Why could not a few local ministers get together in fellowship themselves, and then get some of their laymen fired up with the idea of meeting together? We ought to blanket this country and the world with small groups of praying, experiencing, articulate, trained, and determined people.

Third, this cannot and will not be done without the direct intervention of the Holy Spirit. We must learn more about Him, not from reading so much as by being with people who are led by Him and discovering and knowing Him in action. Too long has the Holy Spirit been to us a doctrine, a vague essence, something—God forgive us!—like an immaterial pigeon which we do not understand at all.

We remember the coming of the Holy Spirit upon the apostolic community on the day of Pentecost, fulfilling Christ's promise and prophecy, and enduing that little beginning Church "with power from on high." What He did in that age is recorded in The Acts of the Apostles, and in the Epistles. What He has done since is recorded in the little-known but often inspiring history of the Church.

It is fashionable today to run down the Church, and often

Christians themselves seem afflicted with a bad case of self-flagellation. It will always be true that when you consider the power to which we in the Church have access through the Holy Spirit, our accomplishments seem meager. But meager or not, these are the events that keep faith burning bright and provide the most helpful signs for the days ahead.

Let us think, then, about God's answer to this time. We begin by remembering how finite are our minds, and how impossible it is for us to fathom either God's mind or His power. We cannot possibly know either God's full will for this world, nor what human forces there are that He can call on and work through in our time. But if we believe that He is "the God and Father of our Lord Jesus Christ," we must believe that the salvation of all men through Christ is His will, that the blessing of all peoples with an opportunity for a satisfying life is His will, and that human freedom offers the greatest human blessing that we can have, and therefore this is His will for mankind.

14.

AN ANSWER FOR OUR TIME

THE QUESTION OFTEN ARISES: Why does not God do away with evil? He has the power to do it—why doesn't He?

It is not as simple as that. A world without evil would be a world without choice, and people would be things and not men. God gives men freedom to act and decide—to sin if they will, to obey His laws if they will. An enforced obedience would be no obedience at all.

When people who profess faith in Him fail to act out that faith, you get what we have on a wide scale today: chaos, conflict, disorder. If Christians had been as busy about the kingdom of God as Communists have been about spreading their cause, or businessmen about selling their products, the situation would be different. There is an unbreakable law: "Whatsoever a man sows that shall he also reap." God does not give us cheap dispensations from meeting the full effects of our actions.

Dr. Perry E. Gresham, of Bethany College in West Virginia, has said, "Only a great religious awakening can save Western civilization. The powerful challenge of the Communist world could be met if there were enough moral and spiritual strength within our society."

Do we believe such an awakening would save our society and civilization? Surely it is worth saving, for there are values in our society that must be preserved if life is to be even tolerable.

A more pertinent question is: Can the Christian forces gather themselves together and work to help the world that is still free to continue its freedom? There are some things that need to happen, and might happen, if all of us realized fully the danger and were ready to accept personal responsibility to bring about an answer.

As intimated in the previous chapter, we must go deeper spiritually ourselves, know the content of our faith, and become carriers of that faith. And, as we have also said, we need a vast program of the simplest kind of lay training. We must learn how to talk about our faith intelligently, relevantly, attractively. That is why the small group, in which such talk becomes increasingly natural and convincing, is of such overwhelming importance.

Whether this begins as a discussion group or as a prayer group, people learn in such meetings to express their convictions. In an article in *Faith at Work* magazine, Billy Graham said:

> One of the definite movings of the Holy Spirit that can be discerned as one travels throughout the world is 'little groups' of 'called-out ones' meeting here and there, dedicated, disciplined, and ready to sacrifice their very lives. I have noticed at various church conferences and retreats that the emphasis is increasing toward the 'house church' in many parts of the world. Perhaps the Holy Spirit is getting His Church ready for a trial and tribulation such as the world has never known.

There could come a time when only in such informal and even secret ways could the Church meet at all. But if we were better trained in our faith and its expression, we should be more ready both for witness to others and for any dangerous days of persecution that might lie ahead.

There is another thing that must happen, and that is the stiffening of our convictions. With this will come the courage to voice them, especially as they concern human rights.

Albert Camus, not a Christian but a man of immense moral conviction and integrity, wrote a remarkable book called *Resistance, Rebellion, and Death.** One chapter is entitled "The Unbeliever and Christians," in which Camus speaks at a certain monastery. First he says he will not be guilty of being a lay pharisee who asks more of Christians than he asks of himself. But he says he shares the Christian's revulsion from evil, by which he means especially cruelty and particularly cruelty to children.

Then comes this magnificent paragraph:

> What the world expects of Christians is that Christians should speak out loud and clear, and that they should voice their condemnation in such a way that never a doubt, never the slightest doubt, could rise in the heart of the simplest man. That they should get away from abstraction and confront the bloodstained face history has taken on today. The grouping we need is a grouping of men resolved to speak out clearly and pay up personally. When a Spanish bishop blesses political executions, he ceases to be a bishop or a Christian or even a man; he is a dog just like the one who, backed by an ideology, orders that execution without doing the dirty work himself. We are still waiting, and I am waiting, for a grouping of all those who refuse to be dogs and are resolved to pay the price that must be paid so that man can be something more than a dog.

Camus sees the battle, which he calls "dialogue," joined between the forces of terror and the forces of reasonableness. He thinks we may see the "sacrifice of Socrates" repeated. But, he asks, "Will Socrates be alone and is there nothing in him and in your doctrine that urges you to join us?"

* Translated by Justin O'Brien (New York: Alfred A. Knopf, Inc. 1963). Quotations are from pages 53-54, 55, 56 of the Modern Library Edition (New York: Random House).

He goes on:

> It may be, I am well aware, that Christianity will answer negatively. Oh, not by your mouths, I am convinced . . . [it is] more probable that Christianity will insist on maintaining a compromise or else on giving its condemnations the obscure form of the encyclical. Possibly it will insist on losing once and for all the virtue of revolt and indignation that belonged to it long ago. In that case Christians will live and Christianity will die. . . . if Christians made up their minds to it, millions of voices . . . throughout the world would be added to the appeal of a handful of isolated individuals who, without any sort of affiliation, today intercede almost everywhere and ceaselessly for children and for men.

That speaks to us all and judges us all. We easily condemn the Nazis and the Communists. Do we condemn the practiced discrimination right here in our own country, or raise a telling voice against it? We count the cost, we keep silence, we forget the rights of others and damn our own souls. I am sure a part of God's answer to our time is a greater indignation, spoken and enacted, against all kinds of inhumanity to man.

But these two things—real lay-training and the stiffening of courageous conviction—are but footnotes to the one real and true answer of God to our time.

I am sure that what we need most, what we should be thinking about and praying for all the time, is a fresh descent of the Holy Spirit upon His people. At Pentecost was revealed an almost absolute spiritual power. Coming upon men whose lives had been changed and fired by the immediate presence and teaching of Jesus, the Holy Spirit gave to them capacities beyond their normal capacities, wisdom beyond human wisdom, power beyond human power, so that they set in motion one of the most remarkable movements of all time, a movement that has never stopped.

There have been long periods when the Holy Spirit seemed nothing more than a doctrine. He is the hardest to describe, the least known of the Persons of the Trinity. We can say that the Father is behind our religious experience, or that Jesus Christ is. But the peculiar power that motivated the Early Church seems generally ascribed to the Holy Spirit. And when Christian faith begins to be an experience and not merely a tradition, He becomes the One of whom we think most when it comes to current, living faith.

15.

THE "FELLOWSHIP OF THE HOLY SPIRIT"

WE SHALL NEVER UNDERSTAND the Holy Spirit theologically nor spiritually until we realize that faith in the Trinity is the complete Christian faith, and that we are not fully Christian, in the sense in which the Early Church was Christian, until we have come to a faith in God the Father, and in God the Son, and in God the Holy Spirit.

This seems to be a kind of progressive revelation. We characteristically believe first in a Creator, then in Jesus Christ who came as an historic figure into the world, and then in the Holy Spirit who came at Pentecost. As you cannot stop at the end of the Old Testament and not go on to Christ, so you cannot stop with Christ and not go on to the Holy Spirit—not if you are going to be a full-fledged Christian. This is not only a theological necessity, it is a spiritual one. We are not equipped as God seems to want to equip us until we are given the Holy Spirit, as individuals and as a Church.

I do not know a better way for us to understand the faith of the early Christians in the Holy Trinity than to consider such a verse as II Corinthians 13:14, where St. Paul first wrote the words so familiar to us: "The grace of the Lord Jesus Christ and the love of God and the fellowship of the Holy Spirit be with you all" (RSV).

God the Father's love, Jesus Christ's grace, the Holy

Spirit's fellowship—here are the precious and sacred threefold blessings. The more you look at them, the more inspired they become, as if Paul had touched on the one great significance for us of each Person of the Trinity.

The Holy Spirit has always been looked upon as God in His relation to the Church. The fresh, continuing, enlivening, awakening, guiding, empowering action of God in and upon and through His Church is the action of the Holy Spirit. He is, in Archbishop William Temple's words, "the God with whom we are all in daily intercourse." The God we know through Christian revelation and Christian worship is God manifest in the Holy Spirit. Some of us for years have been trying hard to give theological allegiance to the Holy Spirit, which, in a very real sense, we shall never do until we experience Him. How do we experience "the fellowship of the Holy Spirit"?

First, let us remember that, properly understood, the Church is itself "the fellowship of the Holy Spirit." To the Church the Spirit was given. By the Spirit the Church lives. Whenever we come into the true Church, we experience something of this fellowship. But it is not something we can catch and hold once and for all, like the color in stained glass windows. It is something more like wind which comes and goes, or like fire which burns up and then burns down.

The Holy Spirit comes when He will. He is given to each of us at our new birth, and is forever after with us, when we are seeking Him, responsive to Him, obedient to His notions. We have felt Him powerfully present in our worship, and we have known barren hours when we were just "going through the motions." Yet even then words of His truth were being said that He might use with someone. He is sometimes present when we are not especially aware of Him emotionally. But I think the Church needs constantly to pray to Him and for Him, that we may be more and more "the fellowship of the Holy Spirit."

Secondly, we experience "the fellowship of the Holy Spirit" in various kinds of smaller companies that are often a kind of "church-within-the-church," the "ecclesiola in ecclesia." The company at Pentecost was not a large company, and perhaps we more often make this discovery of the Holy Spirit in a company when it is not too large. The people in the group need to be very intent on God, not on the form of what they are doing.

Scholars believe that here St. Paul was not praying "for the companionship of the Spirit with individual believers, but that the Fellowship which has been created by the Spirit may continue, along with the grace of the Lord Jesus and the love of God" (C. S. Anderson Scott in *The Spirit*, ed. Streeter *et al*).

This means that he is praying that the believers to whom he was writing might be sustained in the fellowship which the Holy Spirit had created, beginning at Pentecost. These early Christians believed, of course, in God. They believed in a Christ who had died and been raised again from the dead. They believed in a Holy Spirit who came upon their central company on the Day of Pentecost. It was an intensely personal, and also a thoroughly corporate, experience. They were led to believe that this was a permanent gift to the Church, intended to continue for all time.

Robert Barclay, one of this country's early Quaker theologians, wrote:

> Not by strength of arguments or by a particular disquisition of each doctrine . . . came I to receive and bear witness of the Truth, but by being secretly reached by the Life. For, when I came into the silent assemblies of God's people, I felt a secret power among them, which touched my heart; and as I gave way to it I found the evil weakening in me and the good raised up . . . and indeed this is the surest way to become a Christian.

We know that the secret power was the power of the Holy Spirit amidst a quiet, waiting company, attentive to Him and responsive to Him.

We might say that this fellowship exists in three rings. The outer ring is knowledge of each other, names and occupations, looks and personalities, acquaintance and friendship. The second ring is the deeper knowledge of how each one thinks, feels, reacts; what he faces and what interests him; a growing feeling of being at home with him, comfortable, at ease. The third and innermost ring is the bond of long-range, perhaps lifetime fellowship—friendship lifted up to God to be used and infused by Him; joys and sorrows gone through together; a creative, Spirit-filled love. It goes without saying that such fellowship cannot exist apart from prayer, and that every company that prays deeply together experiences something of it.

Spiritual movements begin most surely in this way. Once I met with a group of young businessmen who looked forward to starting something among their own friends. We discussed ways and means. Finally we decided that in the spiritual order the organic comes before the organizational, and while the organic can use the organizational afterwards, it is seldom likely that the organizational alone will create the organic.

We began "letting down our hair" a little with each other, one and then another telling of how God first began to come to him. Our experiences were varied but all quite similar when brought together. We had, I think, a sense of something quietly being born among us: the Spirit seemed to be guiding us as a company from a wrong to a right approach, from a large to a small one.

We need continuing, experimenting small groups where the Holy Spirit may lay hold of a group of people, win them, train them, and use them for His service. I go so far as to say that without these informal, experiencing little gatherings of people, our churches can grow formal to the point of stagnation, and have repeatedly done so. On the other hand, without the balance of the Church with its historical and theological perspective, the informal groups can dissipate into mere nests of subjectivism.

It is my own belief that the "fellowship of the Holy Spirit" is not only the one answer to these needs, but that the characteristic way in which the Holy Spirit is revealing Himself to a lonely generation that longs to belong is in the small, informal fellowship, where exchange of ideas and experience, concern and prayer, are the basis of coming together. Wherever there is spiritual awakening today, you will find people coming together in these little companies which both signalize awakening and set it forward.

Third, we find "the fellowship of the Holy Spirit" where the Word of God is being preached to people within and without the churches. The continuation of the Pentecost story in Acts 2 shows us the fellowship in action together. It says ". . . Peter standing with the eleven lifted up his voice and addressed them. . . ." Notice that Peter did the speaking as for the company of the apostles; he did not do it alone.

Every man who preaches the Gospel will give his own slant to it, but he must keep to the great themes and the common truth. He will be more effective the closer he is to a company of praying, inspired people. When there is prayer, expectation, and a great love for God and for people, the Spirit may lay hold of a man and use him in wonderful ways.

The Spirit speaks in currents of spiritual power, not only through articulated words. Someone told me of a group of deaf and dumb people who went to one of Billy Graham's meetings in New York. Their interpreter was facing them, with his back to Billy Graham. He seemed able to convey through sign language the message that was being given on the platform. These afflicted people understood it, felt it, grasped it, and a proportion of them went forward to a Christian decision. It seemed to me a touchingly vivid modern counterpart of those who, at Pentecost, "heard them telling in their own tongues the wonderful works of God."

How many of us have any adequate conception of the desperate need and spiritual hunger of the world—a need that can be satisfied only by the Gospel of our Lord Jesus Christ? Do we have any sense of our spiritual failure, as a Christian Church, to begin to meet that need? What we are doing is peanuts compared to the need!

If businessmen or statesmen saw an economic or political need and vacuum as great as this, they would find ways to fill it, you may be sure. With all our manpower and equipment, we could do twenty times what we are doing if we wanted to badly enough. If we were a real "fellowship of the Holy Spirit," we should more nearly match what the Early Church was and did.

We have heard much of the Holy Spirit as the Comforter. Let us pray that for us today He may be the Holy Spirit, the Dis-Comforter, who will make us positively miserable until we are doing more for Him through His fellowship.

16.

EVERY MAN A PROPHET

FOR A LONG TIME I felt that "prophecy" was a difficult subject to handle. I thought it had to do only with prediction, which seemed a dubious exercise, fraught with the possibilities of error. Prophets were not like other men; they were extreme.

Historically, this is a false picture of prophets. The Hebrew prophets were not so much concerned with foretelling the future as with forth-telling the truth of God as it impinged on the life of their day. Their predictions had to do mostly with what was going to happen if people continued to disobey God.

They emphasized God's holiness and fearlessly criticized contemporary life. They lived among the people, though there were sometimes schools of them living austerely in a community. They rebuked kings on occasion, as Nathan rebuked David, and castigated the selfish rich.

There has never been another period in history quite like that covered by the five hundred years of Hebrew prophecy initiated by Amos about 750 B.C. These men did much to move Israel to its then unique monotheism, and to make the people of Israel the spiritual pioneers of our race.

Prophesying did not go out with Christ and the New Testament times. Jesus had much to say of prophets and was Himself called one of them. He also said that prophets would not be without honor save in their own country.

Everywhere the prophet sees deeply into the spiritual significance of events, and "has his say" fearlessly as God guides him to say it.

In the first letter to the Corinthians, chapter 12, St. Paul talks about spiritual gifts. "To each is given the manifestation of the Spirit for the common good," he says.* Then he enumerates such gifts: the utterance of wisdom, the utterance of knowledge, faith, healing, working of miracles, prophecy, ability to distinguish between spirits, various kinds of tongues, and the interpretation of tongues.

He digresses (chapter 13) to point out the need for charity as the greatest gift of all and the most needed in the Church. Prophecy will pass away, tongues will cease, knowledge will pass away. Faith, hope, and love abide, and the greatest of these is love. This concerns our basic attitude toward God and toward people.

Then he begins chapter 14, "Make love your aim, and earnestly desire the spiritual gifts, especially that you may prophesy." He makes the contrast between speaking in tongues (evidently much sought after in those days as a sign of the Spirit's presence) and prophesying. Paul admits that the people who speak in tongues speak to God, but men cannot understand them. He who prophesies, however, "speaks to men for their upbuilding and encouragement and consolation . . . he who prophesies edifies the church" (verse 4).

Let us see what the function of those who prophesied was. "He who prophecies speaks to men for their upbuilding and encouragement and consolation" (verse 3). He is not impressing people with his scholarship, not delivering a long and eloquent discourse; he has in view the *needs* of his immediate hearers.

These people were all new at the Christian calling. The in-

* This and the following quotations from I Corinthians are from the Revised Standard Version.

sight of someone even a bit further down the road could be a benediction at the right moment. They needed to know how others were taking the inevitable persecution. There is always a risk in real faith. We need sympathy, the right hand of others walking the same way. We learn from each other when we are in the crucible of actual, living experience.

". . . if all prophesy, and an unbeliever or outsider enters, he is convicted by all, he is called to account by all, the secrets of his heart are disclosed; and so, falling on his face, he will worship God and declare that God is really among you" (verses 24, 25).

What was going on to cause such effects? These people must have been speaking "heart to heart," so that it was like stepping into a current to join them.

The outsider "is convicted" by what he hears–it hits him where he lives, and he knows he should be doing the same thing. He is "called to account"–he knows he has an obligation in this world to settle. "The secrets of his heart are disclosed" — others have dared to consider things he has never considered, and somehow they bring his secrets to his mind. "And so, falling on his face, he will worship God and declare that God is really among you." If you have seen anyone under a profound religious conviction, you know this is not an exaggeration of what can take place.

What has touched the man? The honesty of these people, I suspect–and their reality of faith, as well as the reality of their relationship to each other.

The Early Christians did not admit outsiders at once to their most sacred mystery, the Holy Communion, but apparently they were altogether happy to have them attend a gathering such as this. So the prophesying was to build up those already believing, and to win those who came in to see what was going on.

What did they do at these meetings? Paul says, "When you come together, each one has a hymn, a lesson, a revelation, a tongue, or an interpretation." We do not know what the hymns were; possibly those with poetic talent were already putting Christian truth and aspiration into verse.

Dr. Marcus Dods, commenting on this chapter, says:

> The chief distinction between the services of the Corinthian Church and those we are now familiar with is the much greater freedom with which in those days the membership of the Church took part. . . . Each member of the congregation had something to contribute. . . . The experience, the thought, the gifts, of the individual were made available for the benefit of all.

He cites early hymns, exactness of thought about doctrine, the sharing of the conflict with the world about them, as instances. "And so," he goes on, "passed the hours of the meeting without any fixed order, without any appointed ministry, without any uniformity of service." And then, coming to our day, he comments, "We lose much of what would interest and much that would edify by enjoining silence upon the membership of the Church."

If we are familiar with this letter to the Corinthians, we know that there was danger in too much freedom. Some official leaders needed to be appointed, and some rules laid down. In the public expression of religion there needs to be a balance. The balance of order is needed to check the excesses of freedom. But *we* need the balance of freedom to check the excesses of order! Much of the Church today is dying in decency.

The real truth seems to be that the Christian Church has always had two kinds of gatherings. There has been the formal service, led by regularly constituted clergy, repetitious, liturgical—especially that which concerned the Holy Communion. And there has been the informal gathering, such as you see in the experience of Pentecost, or those we are describing here.

Orthodox churches have gone over almost completely to formal services, and have given no opportunity for the rank and file of members to express themselves on spiritual matters. The balance must be restored. It will not be restored as women are asked only to serve food and raise money, nor as men are asked only to serve on committees and organize building programs.

It is good to break bread together, it is good to take strict care for the institution of the Church, but these alone are obviously not all the Early Church thought important. We must provide other occasions for lay people to express their religious convictions and experiences.

One way is to ask them to speak at formal services. The practice of observing Layman's Sunday has commended itself to many thousands of churches, and this is all to the good. But we need also more continuous gatherings than these. That is why it is so encouraging to see the uprising of small companies of men and women in prayer groups, study groups, and action groups.

You will find in these groups normal, average people like yourself. Shyness and self-consciousness have largely disappeared. Religion has become for them a more natural thing. Speaking more freely of it in a company where faith is either a reality or at least is being sought, they learn much more about how to speak of it with outsiders.

Hearing the experiences of others, they are less surprised at "dry" times in their lives, and encouraged to find what others have found helpful. They are in the process of becoming familiar with basic Christian beliefs and experiences. They have begun to try faith experimentally, sometimes for the first time. A book to read and study together may provide a continuing link for their discussions, but the chief thing is that they are experiencing the things they talk about.

This, it seems to me, is the ideal way for laymen and clergy alike to find a better articulation of their faith. The implication in I Corinthians 14 is that *many* are taking part in this.

Paul says, "I want you all . . . even more to prophesy" (verse 5). "You can all prophesy one by one" (verse 31).

He also suggests a democratic means of keeping things orderly when he says that "The spirits of prophets are subject to prophets" (verse 32). That is, if we speak truth it will commend itself to others; if error, they will detect it. Here is a good check on individualism.

But the whole process is a check on letting the clergy do all the articulation of the faith, and keeping lay people in a state of self-conscious immaturity. All of us would be stronger, better informed, better equipped in our own lives and better equipped to make faith real to others about us, if we engaged in this ancient practice of meeting together outside the formal church service to exchange views, to learn, to pray, and then to act.

If you are not already in such a company, why not get one started at once? As Moses said (in Numbers 11:29), "Would that all the Lord's people were prophets . . .!"

17.

ARE YOU A CHANNEL?

WHAT WAS IT that gave the Early Church its amazing power? At the time when it was numerically weakest, it was spiritually strongest. Never since has there been quite the same overwhelming manifestation of spiritual vitality. Those first Christians were average men and women. What strengthened them was the outpouring of the Holy Spirit. Can we, today, be channels of spiritual power as those men and women were?

While the experience of the Holy Spirit is often a corporate experience, and never entirely separate from the Church itself, it is also an intensely personal and even individual experience.

In the preceding chapter we discussed briefly the spiritual gifts which characterized those in the Early Church. I believe I am right in saying that these gifts do not refer principally to natural endowments, though they cannot be wholly separated from human abilities, but to those new capacities which the Holy Spirit awakens or creates in Christian converts.

We believe that these individual gifts, or capacities to do something special through the presence and power of the Spirit, are meant to benefit the whole Church. The nature of these gifts shows that in the Early Church were many who did more than just believe, more than worship, more than try to behave themselves. They were channels of spiritual power.

One of the great ways by which many of us can become channels of spiritual power is in prayer. Often our prayers are small and selfish. The people who through prayer become channels of power are concerned to pray for themselves only *as* channels and means, in need of direction and power from God, to be used by Him. Their great concern is for individuals they want to help, causes they feel drawn to support, world affairs they know can be influenced by prayer. Let us forget ourselves and think about God and the other person. Let us forget even our limitations and sins, in awareness of God's love.

I knew a small group of women who believed intensely in God and in prayer. At a certain time the terrible conditions in some of our mental hospitals were laid on their hearts, and they began to pray about them. Not long after, a man whom they knew, a Christian minister in another state, was given clear evidence of bad conditions in a nearby state hospital, and took action that led to a shake-up and a tremendous overhauling of the institution.

A young man earnestly sought God in his own life, and having found Him began praying for his college fraternity. Probably others were doing the same thing. Streams of power seemed to be released, and a movement of the Spirit began in that place.

You may say things like this don't happen through you. Let me ask: Do you have a warm concern for others? Do you hurl your life after your prayers, or do you expect God to overlook your own laziness? Do you desire a good answer, and yet relinquish the desire as Christ did in Gethsemane? Do you know that God's answer may come in a different way than you anticipated? Let us ask God to help us be good pray-ers, people who release His power through their prayers!

Another way of being a channel is in healing. It is wise to be circumspect and cool-headed about some of the claims for spiritual healing, but you cannot minimize the healings in the Gospels, and I do not think you can deny real healings by methods which we do not quite understand.

One hot afternoon in the late spring of 1955, I visited a man in one of our hospitals. He was suffering desperately with acute rheumatic fever which had settled in his right knee. The doctors had tried everything. I felt deeply for him in his distress, and longed to help him.

His wife stood by his bed also, and it came to me to say to her, "You take his left hand and I'll take his right hand, and let us join our other hands and put them on that knee and pray."

We did this. I was not aware of special power, but we both cared, and we both prayed, and he prayed with us. Two hours later, quite unaccountably on physical grounds alone, the pain left him and never returned.

I do not pretend to know all that happened and certainly do not minimize what the doctors did. I only know that Christ promised that if two or more are agreed as touching anything, it shall be done (Matthew 18:19).

Do not fear if you feel you are meant to be an agent in this kind of released power. Examine your motives, put away all thought of being spiritually important, and try to let go of any resentment. With prayer, do not hesitate to put your hands on the arm or forehead of a sick person, praying silently if it is better, or aloud if the person is receptive. You may have more power in your hands than you know. It is God's gift, to be used for His glory and for human help.

A third way to be a channel is through words that inspire faith and bring people to Christ. Most of us have received our faith through the faith of others, communicated to us through their lives and words. All of us can do this to some degree.

Try to forget yourself, put all pride away, and let God love that other person through you. Listen before you talk. Pray that Christ may become real to him. Pray, and say what comes from your heart.

Some years ago a young businessman gave his life to Christ after years of nominal church membership. He saw that Christianity was far more than he had ever imagined, and that conversion to Christ is the heart of it.

That winter he was used to bring five other people to a similar experience. He began to live out his religion in his office, and he has brought about a new spirit in human relations there. He makes no bones about his faith, about praying, about his Christian commitment. His life is sufficiently changed to match his words. It leads into conversations with his associates, and to their beginning to live in the same way.

There are many other ways in which people can be channels of power. We shall never know which gifts are ours until we let God clear the channel through us and begin to use us. We can all be used, if we will let Christ take over our problems, surrender to Him our sins, and ask the Holy Spirit to direct us.

III. Living Is EXPLORATION

18.

THE GOSPEL, THE CHURCH, AND MEN

IN *The New Testament in Modern English*, J. B. Phillips presents Mark 1:14b-17 as follows:

> . . . Jesus came into Galilee, proclaiming the gospel of God, saying,
>
> "The time has come at last—the kingdom of God has arrived. You must change your hearts and minds and believe the good news."
>
> As he walked along the shore of the Lake of Galilee, he saw two fishermen, Simon and his brother Andrew, casting their nets into the water.
>
> "Come and follow me, and I will teach you to catch men!" he cried.

Who is it that can say words like these? The claims that lie behind such a statement are stupendous. Here is a man suffering from delusions of grandeur—or here is a Man who is Himself the message and revelation of God. At the very outset of His ministry, and at the first public proclamation of His message, are found the claims that run implicitly all through the Gospels.

He speaks about "good news." Primarily He is Himself the "good news." The Christian Gospel is not only the announcement that the God of the universe is a God of love, but that this God has come into the world in Jesus Christ. The message is our redemption. There is nothing here for us to achieve, but only to accept. It has already been done for us. The good news is the whole message of the Gospel and our response to it.

Jesus says, "You must change your hearts and minds and believe the good news." Here is the call to repentance on which acceptance of the Gospel rests. Repentance is not only feeling sorry for our sins, and admitting our guilt. It is a change of heart and mind that comes about through new faith.

The change begins within. The old life will not do—a new life in Christ must supplant it. God offers us the Gospel—we must take it with our own hands, as individuals. "Come and follow me," Jesus says to Simon and Andrew, "and I will teach you to catch men." He offers them not just a faith, not just a Lord to believe in, but a practical opportunity—the call of a big job.

The Lord is the center of the Gospel; the Gospel is Himself and what He does and teaches. The Kingdom is made up of the lives and works of people who follow Him; and the Kingdom grows as men accept Christ's call to them.

Why are we hesitant to take spiritual responsibility? Perhaps we know very religious people whom we do not admire. They seem to seek the Church as a kind of refuge. Or their daily lives do not match their religious profession. Or they are narrow, bigoted, dull—and we do not want to be classified with them.

Or perhaps we just don't know enough to feel at home in spiritual matters. We say that professionals make it all too complicated. Why not stick to the Golden Rule and the Sermon on the Mount, and leave out all those creeds and theology and ceremonies?

On a deeper level, perhaps our hearts are divided and our commitment shallow. We think the Church is a good thing for the community; we back it with modest financial assistance, and serve on a committee now and then. But we won't get into conversations with other men who are indifferent or opposed, because we know we are not doing anything like what we should. We have not opened ourselves to deeper spiritual commitment for fear of how far it might carry us.

Yet we know that the Church stands for the most important thing in the world: faith in God, without which life has no final meaning or direction. It stands for brotherhood among men, without which we cannot live together in communities nor on the earth. It stands for freedom and is really its only foundation—and without freedom who would care to live? I know that often the Church seems weak and fearful in the very areas in which it is supposed to lead—but what are *you* doing to help change things?

There are two motions we need to make. The first is from the world and into the Church. The second is from the Church back into the world again. This latter motion means putting the things we hear in church to work in our immediate human relations. We talk about "example," but unless our examples have an edge to them, unless we do things very differently from the general run of people, our example challenges others scarcely at all. If we care enough, those who meet us will soon know it. If we share our concern for Christ and His Church with the same enthusiasm we have for our business or favorite avocation, we will make a start.

May I make a few suggestions?

(1) When you talk with people about religion, keep natural and unpretentious and don't be afraid of humor. You are not there to preach, advise, or criticize. You are growing, too, and not perfect, but there is something you care about intensely, and you want to get it across.

A twelve-year-old girl, the daughter of a minister, brought thirteen families into his church by her own work. She felt the importance of Christ and the Church, and she loved the families of some of her young friends.

(2) Deal in events and persons, not in ideas and denominational differences. Talk about what has happened to you or to somebody else. Keep off controversy, and keep to your own need for Christ, and the world's. A sample is always more effective than a general sales-talk.

(3) When possible, take people where they can see something happening for themselves. Few have ever seen a functioning Christian group, or heard firsthand how someone's life was changed.

A young woman was entertaining her parents, and she took them to one of the prayer groups in her parish. Her father told me later he had never seen anything like it. He was tremendously impressed and eager to start such a group in his own congregation. The germ of contagion was already at work.

(4) Seek for a decision and commitment to Christ. A man who is an industrial engineer in one of our great steel mills and his wife brought a young woman and her boyfriend to a meeting where Dr. John Sutherland Bonnell spoke. The young woman wrote to thank them, saying, "What a thrill and surprise to see so many people together representing Jesus Christ! . . . I guess I need a great inflow of God's love. I am going to take the speaker's advice and pray about it. I hope you will both pray for me, too."

The engineer said, "We did pray, and I am very pleased to tell you that both she and her boyfriend dedicated their lives to Christ. They are now teaching a class of young boys."

A man and his wife, with Christian concern, were God's instruments in this. They have answered Christ's call to come and follow and He has begun to make them "fishers of men."

Does this happen through you? Would you like it to happen?

19.

HOW TO TALK ABOUT YOUR FAITH

NO PRESENTATION of the claims of Christ is so effective as the personal spoken word of someone who is in the process of a living experience of Him. People were never so open to faith as they are now, and they talk about it freely. Our obligation to voice our faith in attractive and persuasive ways is greater than ever, as our opportunities are more plentiful.

What has often passed for "witness" in the past is shopworn and outmoded today. You cannot tackle people with an abrupt enquiry into the state of their souls' health. You cannot quote Scripture to them right off, without preliminaries. Most evangelical lingo is both incomprehensible and distasteful to modern people. A simpler, more natural, and truly unprofessional approach is needed.

I think there are six factors which contribute to the effectiveness of any witness for Christ.

The first—and the one for which there is no substitute— is to be a *gentleman.* I mean this strictly in the sense of having good manners. Gentle people know the "feel" of a situation and are sensitive to other people's feelings.

Most people are eager to impart something personal of themselves, and welcome it when you impart something of yourself, but not if it all comes out at once, before you have established some real relationship. It is better to practice restraint than to gush forth and frighten people.

This kind of gentlemanliness is the refinement which true faith in Christ gives to the human spirit. I know few people who define the word "gentleman" better than does Ralston Young, Red Cap 42 at New York's Grand Central Station. At ease with people, forever putting them at ease, he seems always to say the right thing because he is feeling the right thing—not merely the pat, polite thing, but the word that warms people and brings them out and sets the stage for further exploration of spiritual matters. He did not learn it in college; he learned it from Christ.

The second factor is closely allied to the first. It is the need to have a well-developed *worldly sense.* The Gospel seeks to build a bridge between God and man, a bridge solid on both ends.

We must know how people react, think, and feel. Sentimentality, naivete, the innocence often associated with religious people have no place. It is false saints who simper; real ones are shrewd and realistic.

Christians are needed who have not been taken "out of this world," but who are truly part of it in understanding. To balance this, there must be something in every Christian which is deeply separated from the "world"; otherwise he is so much a part of the problem that he is no part of the cure.

The third factor needed in a good witness is *humor.* I do not so much mean the ability to tell a good story, but rather the awareness that we do not have all the answers, and are sometimes pretty poor at living out the ones we have. Humor, especially when directed at ourselves, is the best way to let people realize that while we take our religion very seriously, we do not take *ourselves* seriously at all!

A good laugh brings us down to earth. It counteracts the "stuffed shirt" quality. Humor tells people, "Take all the sawdust out of what I have said so far; let's begin again."

It creates a new rapport between speaker and hearer. By seeming to step back a pace, we actually move ahead.

How many of you still have a sneaking suspicion that religion and humor don't mix—that you can be humorous until you mention God, but then you must be solemn? This is heresy—but there are thousands who believe it, and by their solemn piety drive people away from the stream of life!

A fourth factor is *humility*. This does not mean the self-conscious cowardice that fears to step up to the bat and take a swat at the ball. That is not humility, but pride backfiring. We fear to fail, to appear foolish.

Humility, moreover, may not be without confidence in what we have to do. It is concerned with whether one believes God is at the center of life and is the Giver of all human gifts and talents. Therefore, if you want to cultivate humility, you had better seek it through gratitude. Gratitude is the best offset to pride, and the surest source of true humility.

The fifth factor is the *honesty* that tells of your own experience, and of Christ who caused it. This is what you have been aiming for all the while, but if you come at it too early you lose people. It is not until they find they can trust you, that you are not a religious fanatic or "phony," that people will listen when you say something personal. If they have seen good manners, knowledge of life, fun, and simplicity in you, they will be disposed to listen when you come to the point.

A blunt, premature declaration of faith will scare them off and close them up. If you are with them personally, there will be exchange and getting to know each other, and you will be watching for reactions and needs. If you are speaking publicly and there is no occasion for this personal interchange, they must feel you are the kind of person with whom they could talk and be at ease.

You will then get into human problems, beginning with

some of your own, about which you will talk naturally and in some detail, moving on into what Christ has done for you in facing and resolving them. This evokes an almost automatic response. It may be such a strong response that people are made uncomfortable and want to run away. Or it may be such that they want to stay behind and talk.

The progression in this part is, I think, threefold: human needs, the answers we are finding to human needs, and Christ who holds the answers.

But there is something else that goes into a good witness because it is inseparable from a full Christian life. That is *joy*. It is the first thing people see about us, or else miss in us—the joy of discipleship.

Some are "joyous" only when they can forget their religion and do as they please. True joy lies in loving and serving Christ. If you have it, you can't hide it. If you haven't got it, you can't fake it.

This joy is what first impresses other people, and lingers longest with them. Ralston Young says of the old woman who first turned his mind toward spiritual things: "She had gaiety. She was a live wire. Buoyancy, that's what I mean—it's bubbling!—never a dull day."

I think this joy marks the unmistakable presence of the Holy Spirit. It is akin to enthusiasm. It is more than a buoyant disposition, and is often found in quiet people. This joy is aware of God much of the time, and of His working and presence, and of the coincidences which seem to go along with faith.

We are all meant to have it, and can hardly be good witnesses without it—the joy of being in the stream of God's power. Joy, I suspect, is the most attractive quality in the world.

Jesus said about Himself: "The Son of Man came, enjoying life, and you say, 'Look, a drunkard and a glutton, a bosom friend of the tax collector and the outsider!' " (Luke 7:34, Phillips' translation).

The force of that passage would be lost if Jesus had been an ordinary worldling. But His attitude is not common among those who are serious about religion. Jesus was utterly committed to God and His enterprise in the world, yet He enjoyed life and went so often with people who ate and drank too much, with tax collectors and with pagans, that they accused Him of being one of them.

What a wonderful badge and accusation! What a pattern for modern people to follow! "Enjoying life"—when have you heard this as a recipe for witness to religious faith? Well, it comes with the best accreditation in the world. It comes from Jesus Christ.

20.

THE OTHER SIDE OF GOSSIP

WHEN ONE BEGINS TO TALK about making faith real to other people, the question always arises, "Isn't example enough?" Example is essential, but it is insufficient. If we accept Jesus' invitation to follow Him and then to become "fishers of men," we will need far more than a good example. We will need to "go and tell."

Until we have experienced faith and let it change and transform our lives, there is nothing to tell. And unless I am more controlled in my emotions, more unselfish, more courageous, more plainly in touch with God than I would be without faith, then I cannot give a very effective witness for Christ.

My example is seldom heroic. But the important thing is not myself, but Christ: not whether I believe exactly what I should, or always behave just as I should, but whether He is the center of my life.

How can a mere human example convey to people anything about who the Lord is, or anything about His divinity, His crucifixion, His resurrection, His lordship over all men? He must make a difference in our lives, and this is vastly beyond example. We must give witness to *Him.*

I am sure that we have to bring people within the range of the living power of Christ today. Note that I do not say within the range of Christian *belief*, but of the *power* of

Christ. Before we know Him directly, many of us know Him indirectly through what He has done for other people. An ounce of experience is worth a ton of argument.

That is how members of Alcoholics Anonymous work. They meet and tell others what it was like when they were drinking, how the message of AA helped them, and what has happened since. Sometime in your life, if Christ is real to you, there was a turning over of yourself or of some big problem to Him, and this made it possible for Him to offer His solution. You had to "let go," so He could take over.

This kind of conversation, carried on in a natural way, stirs and awakens interest. In such an atmosphere, people begin opening up about their own problems: they can't sleep without pills; they worry about a child who is not doing well in school; they can't get on with somebody in the office; they feel bewildered and fearful.

Let them talk. Don't talk too much yourself. Harry Emerson Fosdick said that a man is like an island: you sometimes have to row all around him before you find a place to land. The place we are most likely to find God and faith is the place of conscious needs and recognized problems. You get a person's interest at once if he understands that he is not confronted with an impossible demand to be "good" or to believe something he doesn't think is true.

All right. We see the problem and are in good rapport with the person. What next?

We must help him to commit his problem to God. Self-surrender is the crossroads which every life ought to pass. William James called it "the vital turning point of the religious life."

The vast majority of us who call ourselves Christians go along with about one tenth of us given to God and the rest kept for self. Our best friend is the one who helps us give over the other nine tenths to God in a willing act, involving the decision to have done with conscious wrong, to make amends if we can, and to live henceforth with love toward people and obedience toward God, so far as we are able. We help others to consider the factors which compose that decision, and then make it. No other service we can do is half as important.

In my parish in New York was an old-fashioned gentlewoman, very shy and retiring. I discovered that the grace and humility of her life had come from meeting a Christian woman from India years before, who had brought her to a definite Christian commitment. But she had never thought of going beyond this and bringing anyone else to such a commitment. I told her half-jokingly that she was a spiritual miser.

One evening at a small gathering at my house, I asked her privately if she would like to say something of how she had become a Christian. She was well past sixty and had never spoken publicly in her life. But at a quiet moment in the gathering, she rose to her feet and with some diffidence but more courage told of her experience and what it had meant to her.

Afterward, two women spoke to her and asked if they might discuss the matter further. That was the beginning of a stream of people that continued all through the years until she died. She became one of the most effective people I ever knew, in spite of all the diffidence and conventionality she had to overcome!

A brilliant young Jew, who had taught at Harvard and Princeton, married a Christian girl. Her life impressed him. He wished he had her faith, but he needed intellectual help in finding it. I gave him various books.

One day he told me he was "hung up" on some theological point or other. I said, "I wonder whether it isn't the issue of Jesus, who He really is, that is the difficulty." We talked about the claims of Christ as we find them in the Bible. He read and thought some more. Finally he came back asking to be baptized and confirmed.

His wife's example had impressed him, but it wasn't until he was able to talk things out and think them through, that he reached a decision.

It has been a great part of my life to see people brought into the Christian faith who then begin to bring others into it. They are not superhuman salesmen, but ordinary men and women, students, working people, businessmen, housewives. They have pushed off from the shore of safety and convention, and launched out into the deep of experiencing faith in action and then drawing others into it. There is no way to tell people how to do this. If you are full of it yourself, it will overflow, as good nature and good humor will.

Begin lifting the level of your gossip. Gossip is usually talk about people. If we would refuse to gossip about the wrong things, and start to gossip about the right things, we could begin the conversion of the Church, which would begin the conversion of the world. Gossip constructively, about where you see your own faults; about people who have found faith and are putting it to work. Let God use your tongue.

And then remember that enthusiam is always attractive and contagious. If you love Christ and His Church and what He is doing for you and others, and talk about it with that outward sparkle which is the mark of inward reality, people will catch it and want what God has given you. If you capture their imagination, you will soon capture them.

21.

CASTING NETS AND CASTING STONES

JESUS' INTENTION was always to redeem, not to reject—to convert, not to condemn.

We must grasp this if we are to grasp the Christian attitude toward wrongdoing. In our merciless and stupid way, we often put people in categories. We feel justified in saying, "She is a meddler," or "He always has to have his own way." There may be facts to substantiate such judgments, but our judgments only damn people and push them back into the categories we condemn!

Christ held no such final attitudes. He knew that people could change, and under right stimuli often did change. His clear eye always saw the situation as it was, but His clear faith always looked beyond the situation to the person's potential.

What he wanted to do was to set in motion the process of transformation. No one who follows Him is allowed to hold a fixed and hopeless view of other people. In judging others, we inevitably judge ourselves. The puritan who looks down his nose at another and does nothing to reclaim him merits the same scorn as the person who has "done wrong."

Some time ago, a certain clergyman was discovered to be alcoholic. He disappeared from his parish, and the rumor got around that he was suffering from "aphasia," but those who knew him were aware that he was on a binge. The other ministers in the town heard what was happening, but when he came back not a single one of them paid him a visit, nor offered to help. Condemnation is certainly implied in such silence and withdrawal!

The man's bishop, however, did something quite different. He said, "If you will tell me just what happened, and join up with Alcoholics Anonymous, and make a clean breast of this with your vestry and people, I will stand by you." The clergyman agreed to this.

Later, the bishop met with the vestry and asked what they would do with their priest. One or two murmured something about "the good name of the church"—as if it would not in the long run give the church a much better name if one of its clergy were converted than if he were thrown out! The bishop asked whether all of them had always lived in such a way as to protect "the good name of the church," and they admitted that they hadn't. They gave the man another chance. A congregational meeting was called, and the same procedure was followed.

For many years thereafter that man remained in his parish —a far better shepherd, we may be sure, than if he had been the victim of a dogmatic, judgmental point of view. Such a story, with its wonderful aftermath, is a perfect illustration of the contrast between the powerless censure of religious Pharisees and the powerful faith of real Christians.

There is a common phrase which says we are to "love the sinner and hate the sin." Dr. Reinhold Niebuhr warns us that this is "not altogether sound morally; and is also psychologically difficult. It is based upon the supposition that the evildoer has been prompted merely by ignorance and not by malice. Yet a very great deal of evil is done in malice; and the proper reaction of anger must include the doer as well as the deed."

I think we must agree that it is not easy to separate the sin from the sinner. The evil deed was first in an evil will, and no man has to keep an evil will nor express it. He can repent of it and change it.

What I hope Dr. Niebuhr meant is that we must dare to keep the challenge before the person. I don't quite like his phrase, "proper reaction of anger," unless he makes it very clear that this anger is provisional and temporary. Jesus was Himself capable of the most tremendous invective when He saw blind self-satisfaction and hardness of heart in professionally good and religious people. Yet how quickly would His mood change if anyone gave the slightest hint of a change on his own part!

Any hardness in us should be ready to melt at once. To keep on with rebuke and recrimination after someone has shown signs of repentance is to play the Pharisee. It should always be in our minds, and sometimes on our lips, "There, but for the grace of God, go I."

Whatever will redeem the person is the right course to follow. We must first ask God to forgive us for personal resentments and unredemptive anger, and then be honest and unafraid to put the challenge. There are times when heedless, irresponsible people must be brought up short, for their own good as well as others'. But we should try to keep so free from bitterness that a real relationship may be maintained. Then the whole process is one whose ultimate intention is redemption.

Our best judgments are partial, and only God's judgments are true. We ought to be growing and changing all the time. It is either sentimentality or despair that makes us leave people as they are, and no Christian should give in to sentimentality or despair; he should know facts and then love redemptively.

In his great book, *In Search of Maturity* (Charles Scribners' Sons), Dr. Fritz Kunkel says,

> The same person, having gone through the amazing experience which changed his hatred into love, may find himself furiously fighting again. Now he fights his former enemies, knowing that he loves them and that he has to change them in order to help them. Thus Jesus fought the Pharisees and the Sadducees, relentlessly and undauntedly. The creative fury of such a fight is the exact opposite of hatred. A fighter who hates is a poor marksman; his hate blinds him. The sacred fury of creative men is the same in the artist's study, on the speaker's platform, and on the battlefield. This fury, originating from the very center of mankind, provides unlimited resourcefulness, endurance, creativity, and often clairvoyance.

Some things, then, emerge clearly about "other people's sins." We reject scornfulness because none of us is in any position to be scornful, being sinners ourselves, and because it is not scorn that befits a Christian, but redemptiveness.

Jerome Ellison, in *Report to the Creator*, says, "To feel the full weight of self-righteousness in our land, one needs to live for a time under the shadow of a shameful charge, well publicized." That's what the alcoholic clergyman lived under. No wonder Jesus said to the righteous and scornful, "He that is without sin among you, let him first cast a stone. . . ."

Casting stones is no business for a Christian. Let us cast nets instead—nets of concern, nets of involvement, nets of caring. With such nets we draw men into the orbit of the great love and forgiveness of God in Christ, mediated through someone who knows from experience what love and forgiveness can mean.

22.

HOW TO LOVE PEOPLE CREATIVELY

HUMAN RELATIONS are the most important thing in the world, next to our relationship with God. Even our faith is of practical importance largely because of its effect on human relationships.

To understand the nature of happy, creative, and responsible relationships, we must understand human nature itself and something of the nature of life. Nowhere is the Christian religion of more value than in providing these essential insights.

In each person there are two selves—something of the angel and something of the animal. Great saints have their peculiar weaknesses—great sinners their peculiar virtues. These qualities not only exist under the same skin, but they seem in curious contradiction; we see in a single person great generosity about one thing, great selfishness about another. We may be lions of physical courage but whining babies morally. We may throw ourselves into a great cause and then let our pride get involved in the success of what began as a purely unselfish enterprise.

If I am not to remain simply a battleground between conflicting forces, something has got to give. I cannot really help myself, for if I could my pride would become unbearable, and I would be worse off than ever. Therefore we need

God. We need Him to change us—not just to help our wills in a battle against our instincts, but to change our attitudes and motivations. Only a person in this process of being changed—possessed of the humility to know he has not arrived and in no position to "correct" or "tell" others—can be of much use in creating mature relationships.

The existentialist Jean-Paul Sartre says something to the effect that we always meet people with a feeling of inferiority and envy, or else with a feeling of superiority and the will to be master of the situation. This sounds cynical, but there is a lot of truth in it. Unless there is a creative overtone in our human relations, something that desires the other person's best interest and not just what I can get out of him (or even what I think is good for him), I shall meet him cringing or crowing.

Many years ago a United States senator was having difficulty with his wife. He had lost a lot of money, and she went on spending what was left as if there were an endless supply. He asked my advice. He was many years older than I, but I said, "Senator, I think that if, instead of talking across a straight line, you two would talk to God first—you would let Him have your fears, and she would let Him have her extravagance."

He finished the sentence himself: "Then she wouldn't put anything over on me, and I wouldn't put anything over on her!" He got the point.

This is true in the relation between husband and wife, between employer and employee, between Negro and white, between Jew and Gentile, between labor and management, between parents and children—between all groups that must get along, yet start with a natural self-interest. Think of every relationship as containing not two factors, but three—you and the other person and God.

We all know that the best relationships are the ones in which there is a measure of give and take. The person who is "always right" is almost always wrong. The person who can laugh at himself and say, "I'm sorry," is growing and can help others to grow.

If we can love people out of the worst of their faults, with patience and perhaps some good-natured banter, then we will begin to know something about creative human relations. Long-range love and faith do wonders, and we must never abandon their healing effect.

But let's face it—there are people who will take advantage of love and faith and the patient approach. What do we do when we run up against real injustice?

As a good doctor may need to hurt before he heals, so we must not fear to grasp a situation realistically. Love does not always mean agreement or approval, but it does mean the will to redeem the person and the situation. Soft people, without the courage to get to the real issue, will often let something run on for years which might have been healed by one good frank session.

I worked once with a very able woman whose habit it was to play off one person against another by telling different things to different people. One day we got all these people together in a room and called her in, and each of us reported what she had said to us privately. The versions conflicted of course.

She was trapped. She pretended to faint, and lay down on the sofa groaning. We let her stay there until she stopped the pretense. When her tantrum was over, she realized that she would have to stop the pernicious and trouble-making technique of talking two (or a dozen) ways to keep people happy—which of course only made people miserable.

So here is another rule: *do not talk two ways.* Politic people may be suave enough to get away with it and make themselves popular, but they do not redeem lives and situations. "The truth shall make you free." We may modulate the spirit in which we say things to different people, but we must say the same thing in essence. Lying simply puts off the day of solution and settlement.

Another thing to remember is that we can do infinite harm if we try, by sentimental gifts and lifts, to save people from the bump that may persuade them they have "hit the bottom." If you keep getting between people and the logic of their own behavior, you will not be a real friend.

God works in many a situation where somebody is miserable as a result of his own faults. How can anybody help someone when an indulgent mother, a rationalizing husband, a sentimental friend keeps bailing him out and paying for his escapades and debts?

People need to find in us the kind of love that is greater than their faults and sufficient for all their problems. We shall face facts with them, understandingly, listening and hearing them out. We shall remember that there is always another side to the story. We shall keep quiet in twenty languages about what people have told us of themselves and their problems. Our caring and love and faith can be contagious. It can come like a breath of fresh air into a home, a business, a social situation.

Because God alone can show us how to deal with people, prayer is essential. The spirit in which we go to people can be more important than what we say, and only prayer can take fear, judgment, and temper from our hearts. God's wisdom is greater than ours.

The creative and redemptive love that comes through prayer is one of the mightiest forces in the world. It is the cumulative testimony of those who see deeply into the problems and responsibilities of human relationships that those most truly close to God are also most truly in touch with men.

23.

RECONCILIATION

THERE ARE OFTEN FLASHES of great insight in the writings of the prophets. Such an insight is found in Isaiah 52:8: "They shall see eye to eye, when Jehovah returns to Zion" (ASV).

The prophet is speaking to his people in exile. He is looking forward to a time of deliverance when they will be back in their own land and city. In this verse—a kind of cry of anticipated victory and thanksgiving—he seems to mean that men will look into each other's eyes with understanding after Jehovah has returned His people to their place after bringing them out of Babylon.

This is a vivid picture of what takes place between men when God is with them. It makes clear that, when God is in command, men find a common mind and a way of reconciliation which they do not find without God.

We can put this schematically. When human beings are in relation to each other as if each were a dot at either end of a horizontal line, their differences have to be worked out on a merely human level. But when their relations with each other are as if each were one base angle of a triangle, with God the apex at the top, their differences and problems are met in the presence and the light of God, with the result that they come to see "eye to eye"—a clear symbol of reconciliation and agreement.

Thus a new factor is introduced into human relations, a

factor unknown to those who think only in secular terms. Such people may use a third party as arbiter, who may be presumed to have an impartial viewpoint. This is the principle behind our judicial system, and it is of great importance. But it is not often that such an arbiter can remove bitterness and self-interest. If these could be removed, perhaps the chief source of difficulty between people would be eliminated.

How much more effective would it be if one or both of the contesting parties could drop a strict adherence to his own viewpoint and realize that there might be another! A personality open to reconciliation is one which is aware of the partialness of human wisdom, and therefore humble and open to other sides of the truth than its own.

Such personalities are needed in all kinds of situations. They are needed in industry, for the know-it-all kind of executive (management *or* labor) is one who makes the wheels grind heavily. They are needed in homes, for the dominating father or mother or child makes life very difficult. They are needed in racial and social conflicts, for they are the people who know something about conciliation and reconciliation. They are the peacemakers, and Christ said they should be called the sons of God.

What will produce personalties like this? People who believe in God, and who turn to Him, believing that He can change men's attitudes and minds, are more willing to give up their own viewpoints and to consider those of others. They look for the possibility that they can persuade the other party to turn to God also, that in the removal of a spirit of antagonism and mistrust, God's better viewpoint may come to both, and they many find unity in it.

What can't be accomplished by remaining on the same horizontal level, trying to effect a compromise or agreement, may be done by taking higher ground, and meeting "up there" where the air is clearer.

This is true in domestic relations. What appears irreconcilable down in the flats of human misunderstanding appears capable of solution within the framework of faith and love that God renews in people. If you believe something false about your husband or wife, and try to tell it to God, it sticks in your throat. If you are hurt about something trivial, and try to make much of it in God's presence, it seems ridiculous.

How many couples sit down with a minister in the course of a year, up against seemingly impossible problems! First one, then the other, talks out the situation. In putting it before someone who even tries to stand for God, trivial things appear more nearly in their true light. The minister mentions the tendency to blame others and not oneself, along with the necessity of facing one's own as well as the other's faults.

One of the warring partners finally sees the point and says something like, "Well, I guess I'm no rose." There is some laughter, maybe a few good tears, and then some prayer, and everybody feels lighter and better. Then follows the honest confession that God has been too much left out of the relationship or it would never have got into this snarl—so there is need for a fresh start, for prayers together, for increased dependence upon God.

It works much the same way in business and the workaday world. When God comes into the picture, both boss and employee have the same Boss! When you look to God, even to the extent of opening a business meeting with prayer, something enters the situation that was not there before. Pride is lowered. Goodwill is increased. There is a willingness to understand and be reconciled.

And there is something more—to the extent that God is in command, people will bring out what they really feel, and there is a sharing of ideas which is the first step toward reaching an agreement. The little fellow is not afraid to speak his piece, because he knows God will help produce fairness in the big fellow; and the big fellow knows that God will help to produce an open mind in the person who may disagree with him. This is not infallible, of course, but it works surprisingly often. Nothing astonishes me as much as the relatively small amount of faith that is required to begin the transformation of business relations.

Something else happens when God comes into human relations. He is the one factor I know that can make men disagree without being disagreeable.

Most progress comes from disagreement. Most good ideas come as a protest against the status quo. The essence of a free society is the right to dissent. But as dissent is the seed of progress, so it is also the seed of conflict. In a democratic society, nothing is more important than the spirit in which we live with each other, where there must always be large areas of disagreement.

We begin by letting the majority win and rule for a time. The minority keeps biting the heels of those in power, and this is fine if it is done in a spirit of fair play and considers the good of the whole. If bitterness and mud-slinging come in, the whole liberal structure is threatened.

In personal as well as in community or national matters, God makes it possible to disagree without being disagreeable. Awhile ago I spent several hours with a man to whom I am spiritually close and with whom I have a deep friendship. We got to talking about the present situation in the world. I found that my viewpoint was absolutely opposed to his.

He believes we are almost if not quite as much to blame as are the Communists, and thinks me politically and economically an old reactionary. I think him a sentimentalist who will not face the facts. We told each other so. We did it without pulling punches. It had not the slightest effect on our spiritual fellowship, except to deepen it, knowing that there was a bond between us much closer than agreement about even vastly important public issues.

We did not see eye to eye on national policy, but we did see eye to eye in our commitment to Christ and in loyalty to each other. Nowadays it is terribly difficult to keep such a spirit. I doubt if it can be done without God.

As we have said, bringing God into a situation is not an infallible means to produce desired results. The Christian approach is always to exhaust every means of peaceable settlement. A Christian will lay his pride in the dust sometimes, if it will show his opponent that he is in earnest about finding an amicable settlement. But what does he do if his offers are rejected, or unfair advantage is taken of them? Then he must seek human adjudication, if the case allows, and trust the process of human justice to find a proper settlement.

There are some divorces that ought to go through. There are some rights, even when they work to our disadvantage, that ought to be exercised. But we must always ask ourselves whether we have first honestly tried the way of reconciliation. We must so act that the doors are left open to further attempts.

The matter becomes far more complicated when it comes to international relations. It is almost impossibly complicated when your opponent has broadcast the fact that he will resort to lies and any other kind of propaganda to forward his ends.

As I see it, we must remember two things in our present situation: (1) America has too little awareness of its own sins. We are incredibly trustful that our money can do almost anything, and we have become materialistic to an unbelievable degree. Our hands are not spotless. (2) In spite of our sins and follies, it seems to have been given us to try to stand for freedom in the world. We seem obliged to accept that role, in spite of our knowledge that we are not worthy of it. America, with all her faults, should not fail the cause of freedom now, whatever may happen to us in the process.

But through it all, let us keep Isaiah's promise in mind. Let us remember that there are men of faith and goodwill in Russia, in China, and everywhere else, and that if we could get to them we should have a deep kinship with them. It is still true that God is the source of understanding and peace. It is still true that "they shall see eye to eye, when Jehovah returns. . . ."

24.

WHAT SHALL I DO WITH MY LIFE?

ONE OF THE MOST THRILLING things about being young is the opportunity to decide what to do with one's life.

There is a wonderful passage in William James:

> Not that I would not, if I could, be both handsome and fat and well-dressed, and a great athlete, and make a million a year, be a wit, a bon vivant, and a lady-killer as well as a philosopher; a philanthropist, statesman, warrior, an African explorer as well as a 'tone-poet' and saint. But the thing is simply impossible. The millionaire's work would run counter to the saint's; the bon vivant and the philosopher would trip each other up; the philosopher and the lady-killer could not well keep house in the same tenement of clay. . . . So the seeker of his truest, strongest, deepest self must review the list carefully and pick out the one on which he can stake his salvation.

If you believe in God, you can hardly fail to believe that He has a plan for His creation and for the world, which latter we generally mess up to such a degree that it is hardly discernible at all. If He has a plan for the cosmos, He must have a plan for the constituent parts of it, and especially for sentient and free men and women.

This is not a will which He is going to impose on us. We are free to seek it, to ignore it, to reject it. It is as if a great architect said, "This is how a building ought to be constructed. I give you the blueprint. From here on out, it is yours to build."

How do we find out what God wants us to do? There are three overall considerations that I think we should keep in mind.

The first is the need of the world of our time. We live in a day of revolution, when a purely selfish view of one's life investment is a kind of treason. As someone has said, America is like a prosperous suburb surrounded by slums. It takes no prophetic eye to see that this cannot long continue. Moreover, the cataclysmic social changes within our own nation, which will continue to take place whether we like them or not, call for leadership, hard work, and responsibility. God seeks for reserves to throw into the battle.

The second consideration is subjective. What kinds of powers and capacities do we have which we can use for God and for mankind? There are few talents that cannot serve the general good if they are not used merely for our own advancement. I have known many people who fought against what might be God's will for them, only to find in the end that it was the very best thing for them, and the thing they most enjoyed doing.

The third consideration is a general one and most important. If God is interested in the world, then He is interested in all of it. There is nothing inherently godless in handling stocks or building bridges, and there is nothing inherently pious in going into religious work. God, if we understand Him through Christ, is concerned with having honest and responsible bankers, lawyers, dentists, teachers, mechanics, housewives, as well as clergy.

If Christian vocation means anything, it means every Christian has a special call, and he is meant to find it, not to drift into something that gives him a living. He doesn't have to see a bright light, or hear a voice from heaven, but he must see a need and hear a call. And the most important factor is that he be within calling distance.

Having said these things, how does one specifically seek to find his vocation—God's will for his life?

First, we must honestly want God's will more than our own. He is not looking for hard tasks to impose on us, but we have made a shambles of the world, and because of our privileges I think God wants us to do more than "our share" to straighten things up.

Second, we must ask God to show us His will. Prayer is the renewal, again and again, of our surrender and commitment to God, in the fresh terms of the moment and the situation. God has a will for your life, and He will reveal it to you if you keep seeking it. Abraham Lincoln said, "I find that when the Almighty wants me to do or not to do a particular thing, He has a way of letting me know it." Even if you don't believe that, give it an honest try.

Third, let your imagination play over the possibilities of various courses of action and their consequences. Don't close your eyes to anything. God may expect more of you than you think you can deliver. Let service be your aim, not success of the common kind: the world is in too dangerous a spot for any more pure selfishness to be added.

Fourth, get all the facts you can muster, and then use your head. Someone has said that what we call "thinking" is often just rearranging our prejudices. Back of the way most of us use our minds is the set of our wills. It is not cold logic that keeps people away from God and His will, but cold feet.

Fifth, talk to some wise people. Talk to people who believe in God and have honestly tried to find His will for themselves. Their words should not be determinative, but they may help. God may say things to us through people, and reveal to us cracks in our own arguments, and potentialities in ourselves of which we did not dream.

Sixth, go ahead and act in faith. When the hour comes for decision, decide. Try the work in small ways if you can't dive in headfirst. Dwight L. Moody said he was led into his life's work not by any special event, but "the more I did the more I seemed to have power to do."

Finally, get into the habit of watching for God's signs and hints. One of the world's great brain surgeons was on a ship called the *Sussex* that sank many years ago. He wrote a friend afterwards, "I thought I saw God's finger pointing to me on the *Sussex* and setting me aside as one who had a work yet to do."

Everyone I know who has honestly turned to God with as full a commitment as he knew how to make, has felt sure he was "met" by God in a living encounter and led into God's will for his life. This nearly always involves some renunciation. The cross can be seen as a big "I" with a minus sign through it. It begins this way for many of us, but it does not end this way. It ends in resurrection, new life, the joy of knowing and doing the will of God. None of us ever does it completely, but we can, if we will, be sure of being on the right road. The will of God is the only safe and satisfying course in this world, and it is the beginning of eternal life.

I hear someone saying, "This is all very well, but I'm not a youngster looking for his vocation. My life is already well organized, and I have responsibilities. I have to stay where I am. What about me?"

Let us examine next the possibilities of working for God through the jobs we already have.

25.

YOUR JOB IN A NEW DIMENSION

PEOPLE OFTEN COMPLAIN that the most difficult place to live out their faith is "on the job."

Christianity seems to develop this way: first the individual finds faith. This is a personal experience. But immediately this affects his personal relationships at home, in his social life, and at work.

Let us say, then, that we need the conversion of individuals, the conversion of immediate relationships, and the conversion of institutional or "situational" aggregates of people. Each person must work in and through the thing he knows how to do.

We are not to try to make preachers out of doctors, artists, farmers, salesmen, and factory workers. But we must help them to function through their work. Our function stops short of telling people specificially what to do in their situations. It is theirs to apply the new faith to the old job.

A boiler-room superintendent in a public utility plant was in charge of a crew of eighty rough, tough, and profane men. Weighing about two hundred fifty pounds, this man ruled with an iron hand, pitting his temper against those of his men. When he accepted Christ, he began to feel that this was not good enough. He started to talk with his men in a friendly way, creating confidence instead of fear and competition. He organized get-togethers at noon hour, where men could talk over plant matters and even their own personal problems.

The control his faith had brought him relayed itself to others. Relations improved, work improved, profanity dwindled. There was not a single industrial accident in that plant for the next seven years!

An advertising man found an experience of God that changed his personal and family life. He knew it should change his business, too. He talked with one or two other employees privately, raising with them the question of a daily get-together in the office before the day started. It was to be entirely voluntary.

They tried it, beginning about fifteen years ago. Every morning a group meets in the office at eight-thirty, and a good proportion of the employees come. They read the Bible for a while, bring up problems and questions of policy, are quiet in prayer. It is almost a strainless office, where more than one person has found God just by going there to work.

A young lawyer was consulted about a divorce by the wife of a man returning from overseas. She was, she thought, in love with someone else. The lawyer started working on the case, but that night, at home, he was praying about it, and he felt God was not satisfied with what he planned to do. Next day when he saw the wife, he told her what had happened the night before. He reminded her of the solemn vows she had taken, and of the cruel selfishness of greeting her husband with a demand for a divorce. He spoke frankly of how God can change situations by changing the people in them. She thought it over, reconsidered, decided against the divorce, and went to the West Coast to meet her husband.

There are many people who need to hear some simple advice: don't divorce your husband or wife; divorce your sins instead!

I knew a man who worked in a power plant in New York City. He was trying to be a Christian and knew he should be getting along better with his foreman, a very difficult person.

One Saturday my friend was painting his house and asking God what to do about that foreman. The answer came, "Love him."

Problem: how do you love a person you don't even like?

The next week he noticed that the foreman was sneezing painfully. "Got a cold?" my friend asked. "No, hay fever," was the reply. Suddenly the worker became aware of dust particles in the air, agitated by some big fans.

"Maybe we could work it out to turn these fans off while you're in this section," said my friend. "Are you kidding?" sneered the foreman. "These guys would never cooperate."

Nevertheless the man got busy talking to his co-workers, they did cooperate, and the foreman's sneezing lessened. His disposition improved, and things started to go a lot better in that plant. Jokingly, some of the men started to call my friend "teacher's pet," but others said, "Never mind. As long as you handle that foreman he keeps off our backs."

What a simple thing, but how far-reaching in its effects!

In one of my parishes the senior warden was president of a big company in New Jersey. Someone gave him a book by General Dobbie, the defender of Malta. He got the idea from that book that if God could help a general through the seige of Malta, He could help *him* run a business in Jersey City.

On a fishing trip he gave a copy of the book to his colleague in the company and asked him what he thought about getting some of the other men together to talk about such things. The colleague seemed open to the idea.

Soon after, the company president got some of his key men together one evening for dinner and told them the story. He asked frankly what they'd think of a regular meeting together, to get the right spirit before they reached decisions affecting the company. One or two objected, but the rest said, "Let's try it." They started meeting together at regular intervals to talk and pray, and it changed the spirit of that company tremendously, with concrete improvements in human relations.

Here is another story, this one illustrating changes that can take place in politics.

A lawyer in middle life found himself with some time on his hands and a great concern for the corrupt politics in the state where he lived. He began to work in the state committee of his party. After a time he was made treasurer. This gave him the opportunity to do something about the high expenses of running for high office which meant that only those of great wealth, or those backed by special interest groups, could be elected.

He raised money in small amounts from many sources, making it possible for the party to back men fit for office. He made friends with the governor, a member of the opposition party, and cooperated with him where his policies were in the best interests of the state.

In all this he was quite disinterested and had no idea of running for office himself. But this kind of unselfish integrity inspires confidence and constitutes the kind of leadership people want. When a vacancy occurred in the United States Senate, he was prevailed upon to enter the race, and was voted into office with the highest majority ever given anyone but a presidential candidate in his state.

I believe business ought to be the main extension of the Church in the world. Your responsibilities and opportunities as workers really go beyond mine as a clergyman, for they give you a chance to help others find God because they happen to work with you. Be honest and loving; tell of adventures of faith in your own life without posing as a saint or a spiritual expert. Your chance to work for God and bring people to Him right on your job is tremendous. Will you use it?

I know this will call for a change in you, as it does in me. Many years ago I was trying to help the son of one of this country's great industrialists. He was drinking heavily and we worked together a long time.

One day I had to say to his father, "Do you know what makes that boy drink? It is primarily your domination of him."

The man was enraged and nearly kicked me out of his office. But an hour later he called me on the phone and asked if he could see me. He came to my apartment, sat down, and said, "I run an empire all day, and it's hard to shift gears when it comes to my family."

"Yes," I said, "I know it must be." Tears came to his eyes as he said, "Unless God helps me, I cannot change."

We knelt down together and the industrial giant sobbed out his prayer—penitence for his willfulness and domination, intercession for his son. Well, God answered our prayers wonderfully. But often the first place for them to be answered is right in ourselves.

26.

WHAT IS YOUR VERDICT?

THERE CAME A TIME in the life of Jesus when He could no longer stay out in the provinces where people were friendly and where His ministry was creating a successful movement. We read, "He steadfastly set his face to go to Jerusalem."

As He went, He took His disciples aside and told them plainly what was going to happen. According to St. Luke, "They understood none of these things; this saying was hid from them, and they did not grasp what was said" (18:34, RSV). St. Matthew says that when Jesus "entered Jerusalem, all the city was stirred, saying, 'Who is this?' " (21:10, RSV). His coming shook the city to its foundations. He came not only to present Himself and His claims right in the heart-city of His people, He came to ask a verdict of them.

Was He mad? Was He a fanatic? Was He a demagogue? This man seemed strangely unfitted to lead a political movement, for from the first He had refused to use political means. He called only to the human heart, and asked the kind of loyalty that is above political interests.

Where did His majestic calm come from—and His moral majesty which could drive the money changers from the Temple? And where did He find the terrifying words of prediction about the end of the Holy City itself, which sounded almost like blasphemy?

Who was this man? A terrible necessity confronted the people. They must decide about Jesus Christ.

What did they do?

For some of them, it was just part of the day's excitement. Maybe they pitied Him a little. Or perhaps they were troubled for a moment, as we are troubled by a terrible headline in the newspaper. Then they put it behind them. They decided to stay out of range.

We, too, do this so easily! We can do it even as we keep on going to church and saying the words of faith—if in our hearts we are running away, running away from Christ who asks a verdict.

Others were no doubt puzzled. They did not run away, but they could not make up their minds. They thought about Him, and debated His claims, and speculated about His source of power.

So many of us carry on an indeterminate debate between faith and unbelief, between Christ and ourselves. We ask for a book that will "straighten us out," but the only thing that will straighten us out is the decision which we fear to make. We rejoice on Palm Sunday, and weep at the cross on Good Friday, but still we stand at the same indeterminate place. We do not make up our minds.

Then there were others who did render a verdict, and the verdict was "No." They knew that Jesus was asking of them a wholehearted loyalty that would line them up with Him and His cause. They counted the cost. It would separate them from the crowd, raise issues in the family, and cost too much in personal dedication, so they decided against Him.

Finally there were those who rendered a verdict, and the verdict was "Yes." They not only joined the crowd which strewed palm branches in the roadway and shouted "Hosanna"—they joined the company which stood sorrowing on a ghastly hillside while three men died in agony. They belonged to that withering little band as it dispersed after Jesus' death, and they took their way back to their homes and their hopelessness. They spent days of bleak despair. Their new-found light failed them almost at the moment it appeared—or so it seemed until the brightness of the resurrection dawned on them and transformed their hopelessness, despair, and failure.

Do you think all will be easy for you if you accept Him? Do not join your voices with the shouting unless you are willing to let your path wind up the sides of Calvary. Do not pledge your loyalty unless you are willing to feel the nails and suffer the shame and the thirst and the loneliness and the forsakenness, even by God! We should have had no Saviour if He had not shared fully our lot.

But these few put their hands to the plow. They were going through with it. Christ asked a verdict of them, and they gave it. The verdict was "Yes."

What is the stirring that Christ causes in our hearts? It is a questioning of our motives and of our lives. It is a dissatisfaction with what we are and with what we are doing. It is an emotion of despair touched with hope. It is a troubled conscience over wrong, and an uneasy spirit that longs for better living. It is the haunting feeling that we shall go on living this half-Christian, half-pagan life till the shadows of death fall round about us. It is the shudder that shakes us when we know that Christ is the truth, and we live for so much half-truth and so many lies.

The city to which Christ comes today is the "city" of your heart and mine. It is a city where there is much professed goodness and much hidden shame. It is a city where we receive Him with joy, then crucify Him with forgetfulness and disobedience.

Why the inescapable issue and challenge of Him? The reason this objective Christ who stands outside us is so unavoidable is that there is already an organic identity between Him and our true selves. St. John says that He "was the true light which lighteth every man." If that is true, He who comes to us from without is the One already familiar to us from within. It is as if God created us with an affinity for Christ that we cannot ignore.

Christ wanted to rule Jerusalem—not politically, but spiritually. He wanted to rule the hearts of His people, and He still does. He is not a dictator who will enforce His will on us, but a Lord who wants us to accept His will freely because it is His will. That is why He asks of us a deep decision, a giving of ourselves to Him in as complete a surrender as we know how to make.

Today is a new day. Christ comes like the sun, up over the crest of the hill, and looks in our direction. We know all too well who He is. He does not press a claim upon us; He *is* a claim upon us.

Will you do today what He has asked you to do for years—become His disciple?

He comes asking for a verdict. What will your verdict be?